Soccer's
Most Wanted™ II

More Sports Titles from Potomac Books

The Beckham Invasion by Andrea Canales

Home Run's Most Wanted™: The Top 10 Book of Monumental Dingers, Prodigious Swingers, and Everything Long-Ball by David Vincent

Soccer's Most Wanted™: The Top 10 Book of Clumsy Keepers, Clever Crosses, and Outlandish Oddities by John Snyder

The Year That Changed the Game: The Memorable Months That Shaped Pro Football by Jonathan Rand

Tennis Confidential II: More of Today's Greatest Players, Matches, and Controversies by Paul Fein

Soccer's
Most Wanted™ II

The Top 10 Book of More Glorious
Goals, Superb Saves, and
Fantastic Free-Kicks

Jeff Carlisle

Potomac Books, Inc.
Washington, D.C.

Library of Congress Cataloging-in-Publication Data
Carlisle, Jeff.
Soccer's most wanted II : the top 10 book of more glorious goals, superb saves, and fantastic free-kicks / by Jeff Carlisle. — 1st ed
p.   cm.
Includes bibliographical references and index.
ISBN 978-1-59797-193-5 (pbk. : alk. paper)
1. Soccer—Miscellanea. I. Title.
GV943.2.C37 2009
796.334—dc22

2008020280

Printed in the United States of America on acid-free paper that meets the American National Standards Institute Z39-48 Standard.

Potomac Books, Inc.
22841 Quicksilver Drive
Dulles, Virginia 20166

First Edition

10 9 8 7 6 5 4 3 2 1

For Andréa and Ben

Contents

Contents

Illustrations

Acknowledgments

As with any book, the list of people who helped bring it to life could make for an entire volume on its own, but there were several people who I couldn't have done without. Special thanks go to my editor at Potomac Books, Kevin Cuddihy, who was willing to take a chance on an unknown author. Then there are those whose help with source material was invaluable. These include Rick Lawes and Will Kuhns for their instant recall of all things MLS; Dan Courtemanche for his help in acquiring information about the WUSA; Jack Hueckel, Roger Allaway, and Colin Jose at the U.S. Soccer Hall of Fame in Oneonta, New York, for their vast knowledge of American soccer history; and John Todd of ISI for his help in acquiring the photographs used in this book. Special thanks also go to Dylan Hernandez for his sage advice.

Introduction

In Nick Hornby's book, *High Fidelity*, the protagonist, Rob Fleming, spends hours arguing with his music store co-workers over "Top Five" lists on various musical topics. *Soccer's Most Wanted II: The Top 10 Book of More Glorious Goals, Superb Saves, and Fantastic Free-Kicks* is intended to be its soccer equivalent, in that it is more than just a trivia book. It's a "Things you argue about with your soccer friends" book, with the topics involved delving beyond the "Ten Best Players of All-Time" type of discussions. Everyone remembers the World Cup winners, but what about the best teams who fell just short? And what about the great players who never got to appear on the world stage? Then there is the burgeoning amount of material relating to the American game, thanks to the steady progress of Major League Soccer, not to mention the strides made by the country's men's and women's national teams. That's not to say there won't be loads of other trivia—and trivial items—to discuss at both club and international level. Beyond the mere facts are some compelling stories from all over the globe.

Soccer's Most Wanted II is also a follow-up to *Soccer's Most Wanted: The Top Ten Book of Clumsy Keepers, Clever Crosses, and Outrageous Oddities.* Like its predecessor, it intends to highlight the crazy incidents and other interesting bits of trivia that have helped make soccer (football to the rest of the globe) the most-watched sport on the planet.

Where this edition differs from the previous book is in its greater emphasis on the American contributions to the sport. Contrary to popular belief, soccer has a rich and at times tortured history in the United States, and there are many interesting nuggets of information that remain to be told.

And, of course, there are those stories that transcend sport. Soccer players everywhere have never managed to stay out of the headlines (or tabloids) for long, and their foibles and infamous incidents are also chronicled in the fifty top-ten lists that comprise this book.

In the Beginning . . . American Style

Given the sheer ineptitude shown by owners of American soccer teams, it's safe to say that P. T. Barnum would have loved doing business with the country's keepers of the beautiful game. But soccer's roots in the United States rival those of other, more storied soccer playing countries. The American Football Association, the precursor to the U.S. Soccer Federation, was formed in 1894, making it the first soccer association to be formed outside of Britain. Of course, since then the history of the game in the United States has become littered with now-defunct professional leagues. Soccer's unmatched tendency for cannibalization, as well as competition from more established American sports are the primary reasons for the game's struggles. Nevertheless, each of these professional leagues has its place in the annals of American soccer history.

1. AMERICAN LEAGUE OF PROFESSIONAL FOOTBALL CLUBS, 1894

The ALPFC's existence was as painful as it was brief. Formed by six owners from baseball's National League, the venture was started as a means of earning revenue in the off-season. Far from being the money machine that it is today, baseball back then was run by owners whose business savvy was suspect, and their mismanagement was a prime cause of the ALPFC's downfall. The decision to hold games mostly on weekdays, when most paying customers were working, is a prime example.

The authorities were later shocked, shocked mind you, that the Baltimore entry had imported players from Britain, and given the then-existing climate of borderline xenophobia, the use of such ringers was a public relations disaster. The owners proceeded to pull the plug on their new venture a scant three weeks after the first game was played.

2. AMERICAN SOCCER LEAGUE, 1921–1931

In the eyes of many soccer historians, the period in which the first ASL existed constitutes the first Golden Age of American soccer. Unlike the ALPFC, the ASL was blessed by owners with better organizational skills. When the British countries withdrew in 1920 from FIFA, soccer's governing body, the regulations governing the international movement of players went out the window, and top overseas performers were free to ply their trade in the budding league. The ASL was initially composed of eight teams in the Northeast, and expanded to twelve by 1924, drawing crowds comparable to National Football League games. With the high level of play, soccer seemed well positioned to grow into one of America's main sports.

So what happened? In 1925, a minor dispute took place between the league and the U.S. federation over the league's participation in the U.S. Open Cup. The teams didn't want their season interrupted by the competition, with the federation insisting otherwise. What ensued was a full-scale turf war. The federation suspended the league, depriving it of FIFA sanction. Teams defected from the ASL as a result, and amid such chaos some of the wealthier owners pulled out. When the Great Depression hit in 1929, the ASL no longer had the financial means to survive, and a tremendous opportunity to advance the game in the United States had been squandered.

3. **AMERICAN SOCCER LEAGUE II, 1933–1983**

From the ashes of the first American Soccer League, a second incarnation emerged two years later, mostly because of the unflagging efforts of New York Americans' owner Erno Schwarz. But the league found itself in a Catch-22. If it was to grow it needed to shed its reputation as a game played and watched only by immigrants. Yet those were the very fans keeping the league in business. Add in the fact that the ASL was never able to attract the kind of deep-pocketed investor who would ride out the lean times, and you had a league that never rose beyond semi-professional status.

The ASL carried on until 1983, but by then a new and better-financed competitor had overtaken it.

4. **NORTH AMERICAN SOCCER LEAGUE, 1968–1985**

Formed by a merger of the National Professional Soccer League and the United Soccer Association, the establishment of the NASL coincided with the second Golden Age of soccer in America. The league at last had some wealthy owners who could effectively finance and market the game. When Pelé signed with the New York Cosmos in 1975, other high-profile players followed, and the NASL experienced unprecedented growth and recognition.

But the foundation of the league was unstable. With the Cosmos buying practically every famous player in sight (including the likes of Franz Beckenbauer and Johan Neeskens), a soccer arms race ensued with other teams buying stars just to keep pace. The result was that teams wracked up huge financial losses. With indoor soccer providing competition for players and fans, and with the league unable to provide additional revenue streams via television, the NASL folded in 1985. The sport wasn't dead, but it was certainly on life support.

5. MAJOR INDOOR SOCCER LEAGUE, 1977–1992

Soccer's indoor variant attained professional status in 1977 through the efforts of Earl Foreman. The league initially achieved a level of peaceful coexistence with the NASL, but like so many times in the game's history, the sport's penchant for self-destruction took over, and Foreman soon aligned his league to be in direct competition with the NASL. Battles for players were soon commonplace, and Foreman openly derided the outdoor game as being "too European."

When the NASL died in 1985, Foreman got his wish, but soon found himself fending off another indoor league called the American Indoor Soccer Association. The resulting competition, as well as the franchise instability that plagued the league for its entire existence, saw the MISL close its doors in 1992.

6. A-LEAGUE, 1990–1996

Following the demise of the NASL, a variety of regional outdoor leagues kept the flame burning for the outdoor game. Included in this group was a third incarnation of the American Soccer League located in the east, and the Western Soccer Alliance located on the west coast. The two leagues merged in 1990, although they essentially remained two distinct entities, with each league's champion meeting in a playoff to determine the champion.

The league was essentially dissolved in 1996, at which

point most of its teams joined the United Soccer League, which went on to use the same name for what was the de facto second tier of American soccer.

7. MAJOR INDOOR SOCCER LEAGUE II, 2001–2008

Much like the outdoor game, the indoor variety has undergone an alphabet soup of leagues since the original MISL closed its doors in 1992. In no particular order, the Continental Indoor Soccer League (1993–97), the National Professional Soccer League (originally the American Indoor Soccer League, 1984–2001), and the World Indoor Soccer League (1998–2001) all came and went. But in 2001, the second incarnation of the MISL was born, with six teams joining from the NPSL, and two teams coming from the WISL. It didn't last however, as the league suspended operations in 2008.

8. WOMEN'S UNITED SOCCER ASSOCIATION, 2001–2003

At the conclusion of the 1999 Women's World Cup, which witnessed packed stadiums and an American victory, the goal of a women's professional league began to take hold. In 2001, that dream became a reality with the formation of the WUSA, but unfortunately an inability to learn from the game's history doomed the new venture.

While the play on the field made the WUSA the premier women's league in the world, massive overspending, along with a lack of ancillary revenue from stadiums, led to crushing financial losses. These were all lessons that previous leagues as well as Major League Soccer had learned the hard way, but they were ignored by the WUSA, and when the league closed its doors after just three seasons, the first and best opportunity for a women's league evaporated.

9. UNITED SOCCER LEAGUES, 1986–PRESENT

The USL initially began life as the Southwest Indoor Soccer League, but under the leadership of Francisco Marcos the organization gradually morphed into an outfit that encompasses the entire base of the American soccer pyramid, with leagues that comprise the second, third, and fourth tiers of U.S. soccer. This structure is vital to the development of American players, who can now play in a professional environment with the hope of one day playing in MLS. The USL also contains the W-League, a semiprofessional women's league that has served to bridge the gap between the WUSA's demise and its successor, Women's Professional Soccer, which is set to begin play in 2009.

10. MAJOR LEAGUE SOCCER, 1996–PRESENT

When the United States was named as hosts of the 1994 World Cup, one of the conditions was the eventual establishment of an American league, and in 1996 MLS was born with ten teams. And unlike its predecessors, the league appears to have finally understood the challenges of selling soccer in America. The league is well-financed while practicing strict cost containment. MLS has also been intent on building its own stadiums, the better to tap into the ancillary revenue streams that other sports take for granted. And on the field, the league has placed a heavy emphasis on developing American players.

It hasn't always been smooth sailing, with MLS folding two teams after the 2001 season. But the league survived that period and is now in an unparalleled position of strength, with new owners coming on board and the league set to expand to sixteen teams by 2010.

The U.S. Open Cup

Imagine a basketball tournament open to every team in the country, amateur or professional. Apply that to soccer and you have what is now known as the Lamar Hunt U.S. Open Cup (USOC), which was named after the late owner of the NFL's Kansas City Chiefs. Hunt was one of soccer's biggest supporters in the United States for over forty years until his passing in 2006. The tournament began in 1914 as the National Challenge Cup, making it one of the oldest professional competitions in the history of American sport. Only Major League Baseball and hockey's Stanley Cup have been around longer, but given the obscurity that soccer has long toiled in, the Open Cup has remained one of U.S. soccer's best kept secrets.

1. INAUGURAL CHAMPIONS

Two New York teams, Brooklyn Celtic and Brooklyn Field Club, contested the first final on May 16, 1914. So of course they had to travel to Pawtucket, Rhode Island, to play the match, although given the fact that 10,000 people showed up, perhaps the organizers knew what they were doing. The match finished 2-1 in favor of the Brooklyn Field Club, and it was their captain, Adamson, who hoisted the Dewar Challenge Trophy (named after Sir Thomas Dewar, the maker of Scotch whiskey).

2. FIRST DYNASTY
It didn't take long for the competition's first dynasty to emerge, as Bethlehem Steel won four of the first six tournaments that were held, and became the first back-to-back winners when they prevailed in 1915 and 1916. They duplicated the feat in 1918 and 1919, before winning the title for the last time in 1926.

3. THE RIOT FINAL
What is believed to be the first soccer riot in U.S. history took place during the 1916 final when Bethlehem Steel defeated the Fall River Rovers 1-0. The only goal came when Tommy Fleming converted a penalty kick in the seventy-eighth minute, but when Fall River had their own penalty appeal denied with just seconds remaining, their supporters invaded the field with referee David Whyte their intended target. The police finally restored order, although according to an account in the *Bethlehem Globe*, it wasn't until "one of the officers drew his revolver" that the crowd was brought completely under control.

4. MOST TITLES
Los Angeles Maccabi shares Bethlehem Steel's distinction of five titles. The club was the dominant team of the '70s and early '80s when the tournament was largely the domain of amateur teams. Maccabi also finished as runner-up on two other occasions, making it the team to have played in the most finals.

5. **WHO ARE THOSE GUYS?**

The Fall River Marksmen suffered from something of an identity crisis in 1931. Prior to that year's ASL season, owner Sam Mark moved the club to New York and renamed them the New York Yankees. But since the team had already been entered into the Open Cup as Fall River, that was the name they went by during the competition.

But an even stranger twist took place prior to the third and last leg of the final. In a scene reminiscent of a Sunday pub league, the Marksmen had only eleven players, but their

The Fall River Marksmen await the presentation of the James P. Dewar Challenge Trophy following their triumph in the 1930 U.S. Open Cup. Standing sixth from right is Billy Gonsalves, who won eight Open Cup titles with five different clubs during his storied career. *From the archives of the National Soccer Hall of Fame, Oneonta, New York*

captain, Alex McNab, had broken his arm in a midweek friendly. He was listed on the lineup sheet and participated in the coin toss, but then took a seat on the bench, leaving his teammates to continue with just ten players. Incredibly, Fall River still prevailed 2-0 over the Chicago Bricklayers, taking home the title for the fourth and final time.

6. BILLY GONSALVES

If there was an undisputed king of the U.S. Open Cup, it was Billy Gonsalves. The son of Portuguese immigrants, Gonsalves began his career in the late '20s during soccer's first heyday. And while he scored his share of goals, he was one of the players who made everyone around him better. Never was this more evident than in his winning eight Open Cup titles with five different clubs. Gonsalves's run started with the aforementioned Fall River Marksmen (1930, 1931), and continued with the New Bedford Whalers (1932), St. Louis Stix, Baer, and Fuller (1933, 1934), St. Louis Central Breweries (1935), and finally Brooklyn Hispano (1943, 1944).

7. GOAL KINGS

The USOC has seen its share of stellar goalscorers, but two performances stand out in the tournament's long history. In 1931, U.S. international Bert Patenaude (who in 1930 recorded the first hat trick in World Cup history) scored five goals in the first leg of that year's final, leading the Fall River Marksmen to a 6-2 win over the Chicago Bricklayers. Nearly thirty years later, Mike Noha delivered another performance for the ages in the epic 1960 final between the Philadelphia Ukrainian Nationals and the Los Angeles Kickers. Noha had already notched a hat trick at the end of normal time that finished 3-3, but in extra time, the Phila-

delphia forward took his game into overdrive, scoring twice
more to give the "Uke Nats" the first of their four titles.

8. CHICAGO FIRE

With the arrival of MLS, full professional teams entered the
USOC for the first time since the '30s. Even then, not all MLS
teams took the competition seriously, with several opting to
play with mostly reserve players. The Fire has taken a different approach, fielding most of their starting lineup in USOC
matches, and their strategy has paid off. Chicago has
claimed four Open Cup titles, the most of any MLS side.

9. ROMA FC

The magic of a cup competition is most keenly felt when a
minor league club claims the scalp of a top-tier side. And
while this has happened on numerous occasions since MLS
clubs began participating in the USOC in 1996, the single
biggest shock occurred on July 12, 2006, courtesy of Dallas, Texas-based Roma FC. Roma was an amateur side playing under the auspices of the U.S. Adult Soccer Association
(USASA), and it had qualified for the USOC after winning a
regional tournament. After upsetting the USL's Miami FC
in the second round, Roma were set to play MLS side Chivas
USA. But rather than take a happy-to-be-here attitude,
Roma battled Chivas to a scoreless tie before prevailing on
penalty kicks 4-2, with goalkeeper Jesse Llamas saving
two Chivas attempts in the shootout. Roma's dream died in
the next round as they fell to the Los Angeles Galaxy 2-0,
but their win over Chivas remains the only time a USASA
side has triumphed over MLS opposition in the USOC.

10. ROCHESTER RAGING RHINOS

One upset is nice, but the Rochester Raging Rhinos delivered a slew of them in 1999, as they rampaged their way to the USOC title. The Rhinos were playing in what was then known as the A-League, the second tier of U.S. professional soccer, but they proceeded to plough through four MLS teams, beating cup specialists Chicago 1-0 in the third round, as well as prevailing over Dallas and Columbus before beating the Colorado Rapids 2-0 in the final. Rochester's victory marks the only time that a non-MLS side has won the tournament since the league's inception.

Tales from the Crypt

The legacy of the North American Soccer League is one that is a walking contradiction. In the years that followed the NASL's death in 1985, some would argue that the league's financial recklessness set back the progress of the game in the United States and Canada. Others would counter that the soccer roots set down by the NASL helped pave the way for the game's eventual revival. Regardless of where one stands in that debate, what can't be argued is that the league did have its share of crazy innovations and memorable moments, making it a joy to watch. Unfortunately, many of those memories have been lost with the passage of time, but enough have survived to help burnish the legacy of what was once American's top soccer league.

1. PELÉ'S DEBUT

June 15, 1975, was a day fit for a king, as soccer's reigning monarch took his NASL bow in an exhibition match against the Dallas Tornado. The venue, Downing Stadium, was far from regal, however. The place was a dump with no running water, save for the overflowing toilets. Grass was another commodity in short supply, so much so that in order to make the field look presentable for television, the groundskeeper spray-painted the field green. As the teams walked off the field at halftime, Pelé looked at his green-hued limbs and became concerned that he had contracted a fungal infection. It took some convincing from Cosmos general manager Clive Toye that medical treatment would not be necessary. Pelé eventually agreed to continue playing, and scored a late equalizer in a 2-2 tie.

2. THE MARATHON MATCH

Americans don't like draws. At least that has been the mantra emanating from soccer's critics for years. And on September 1, 1972, those crusaders were provided with some heavy artillery. The setting was Rochester, New York, where the hometown Lancers were set to take on the Dallas Tornado in the first of a three-game playoff series. Since draws were verboten, the rules stated that overtime periods of fifteen minutes would be played until somebody scored. Sure enough, the game ended 1-1, and what was hoped to be a quick overtime sprint turned into an odyssey. By the time the eighth overtime began, exhaustion had clearly set in. Dallas goalkeeper Ken Cooper had not fully recovered from knee surgery, and when he wasn't making heroic saves he was hopping around the penalty area on one leg. The agony finally ended in the 176th minute, when a shot from the Lancers' Carlos Metidieri rolled over the line. As Dallas head coach Ron Newman related in Clive Toye's book, *A Kick in the Grass,* "It was the only game that I ever remember where both teams celebrated the winning goal." Dallas ended up winning the series two games to one, but not before enduring another epic overtime match that lasted a cozy 148 minutes.

3. THE SHOOTOUT

It wasn't until 1975 that the NASL completely did away

with ties, initially using penalty kick shootouts to determine the winner of drawn matches. But in 1977, a new method, simply called the shootout, was concocted. It involved a player starting thirty-five yards from goal going one-on-one with the keeper. The shooter had five seconds to get a shot off, with no rebound attempt allowed. Purists derided it as the work of the devil himself, but the players by and large embraced the rule, especially since it required more skill than penalty kicks. The rule was later adopted by MLS, until a fan backlash condemned it to the scrap heap, but it's still admired by some players. As NASL veteran Alan Birchenall told David Tossell in his excellent book, *Playing For Uncle Sam*, "The Americans were twenty-five years ahead with that rule."

4. BACK FROM THE DEAD

The aforementioned marathon playoff game wasn't the last time that Ron Newman was at the center of a crazy incident. The Englishman was long at the forefront of selling the game to a skeptical public, and by 1978 he had taken his act to South Florida as coach of the Ft. Lauderdale Strikers. Newman had led the Strikers to a division title the previous season, but when they dropped their first three games of the 1978 campaign, a headline in the local paper asked, "Are the Strikers dead?" In response, the next home game against Los Angeles saw Newman and the players enter the stadium in hearses, with Newman lying on a gurney covered by a sheet. The sheet was pulled back, and in a Monty Python moment, Newman stood up and declared, "We are not dead yet!" Alas, his microphone wasn't turned on, but the crowd ate it up anyway, and suitably motivated, the Strikers won.

5. FASHION STATEMENT

Among the myriad ways that the NASL bigwigs tried to

market the game to Americans was with uniform designs that were in some cases unconventional, while in others downright hideous. The worst of these offenders had to be the uniform design of the Colorado Caribous. Never mind the color choice of brown and tan, the strip of leather fringe stitched across the front and back was something that would make the judges on *Project Runway* gag. Mercifully, the Caribous were in existence for just the 1978 season, one in which they finished with the worst record in the league. The next year they were relocated to Atlanta and rechristened the Chiefs.

6. **LABOR PAINS**

Much of what comprised the NASL was imported, especially the players since league rules mandated that only two spots in the lineup be reserved for North Americans. But one aspect of the league that was entirely homegrown was the labor trouble that marred the beginning of the 1979 season. The players' union, the North American Soccer League Players' Association, initiated a work stoppage for games the weekend of April 14. Unfortunately, the players were about as united as '90s-era Yugoslavia. In some cases entire teams walked out, while others ignored the union's pleas. The result was a farce with some teams importing scab players, while others saw some coaches, including Ft. Lauderdale's Newman and Seattle's Jimmy Gabriel, taking the field. One week later, the teams were back with their full compliment of players, but the response from fans was overwhelmingly negative, especially in a league where teams were universally hemorrhaging money. It was not until 1981 that a collective bargaining agreement was reached.

7. **UNDER THE INFLUENCE**

If there was ever a venue in which the players and fans

could engage in a group hug, it was San Jose's Spartan Stadium. Not only was field width an anorexic fifty-five yards, but the walls ringing the perimeter were only several feet away, making it seem even narrower. It certainly made for an intimate setting, one that Willie Johnston took full advantage of during a 1981 match between his Vancouver Whitecaps and the hometown San Jose Earthquakes. It turns out that Johnston was about to take a corner kick when a fan reached over the railing and offered Johnston a beer. The Scot duly accepted and took a few swigs. Far from impairing Johnston's on-field abilities, he swung in a delightful corner kick that was nodded home by teammate Peter Lorimer.

8. OFFSIDE

Another rule-change adopted by the NASL was the modification of the offside law. For over a century, the rule had stated that a player could only be offside in the opposition's half of the field, but in their never-ending quest for more goals the league adopted—initially with FIFA's blessing—a rule that said a player could only be offside within an area thirty-five yards from an opponent's goal. Now rather than be forced to push up to the halfway line, forwards could camp out more in the other team's half of the field. Reactions by players were mixed. Forwards who relied on pace hated it, as the space behind the backline was reduced. Creative midfielders loved it, as it gave them room to operate. But the group whose opinion counted the most was FIFA, and they later decreed that the NASL needed to play the game like the rest of the world. The league protested, at which point FIFA warned they would turn the NASL into an outlaw league. The NASL finally relented in 1982, and the thirty-five-yard offside rule was no more.

9. THE PARROT BURIAL KIT

If ever there was evidence needed that goalkeepers are an odd bunch, one need look no further than former Vancouver Whitecaps' netminder Tino Lettieri, who before playing every match, would deposit a stuffed toy parrot in the back of his goal as a good luck charm. So following the Whitecaps win over the Toronto Blizzard in the first game of their 1983 playoff series, Blizzard general manager Clive Toye decided to employ some psychological warfare. When Lettieri entered the field for the second match, two men, dressed in black, carrying a shovel and a small box labeled "Parrot Burial Kit," met him. Toye, in his aforementioned book, questions how much the ploy helped, but the Blizzard went on to win the match 4-3. And after sending Lettieri a stack of sympathy cards prior to the series-deciding match, Toronto won the series finale 1-0 and progressed to the next round.

10. FIRST IMPRESSIONS

Almost as nutty as the play on the field were the antics taking place off it, including some notable press conferences, the most memorable of which involved forward Frank Worthington. The Tampa Bay Rowdies had just acquired Worthington in a trade with Philadelphia, and at his introductory press conference, one of the local reporters asked Worthington if he was in America to play hard or if he was on a holiday. At that exact moment, bottles of whiskey and vodka slipped out of Worthington's duty free bag and disintegrated on the floor. Only the faster pace of the reporters' scribbling matched the increased smell of alcohol.

We Knew Them When . . .

The NASL forged its reputation as a haven for has-beens and never-weres. Even the likes of Pelé, Franz Beckenbauer, and Johan Cruyff had played their best soccer elsewhere by the time they arrived, not that it mattered for them. But there were a few players who graced the NASL stage while they were in their prime, and in some cases a few used the league to galvanize their careers.

1. HUGO SANCHEZ

Sanchez arrived in the United States in 1979 as part of a player exchange program between Mexico City-based side UNAM Pumas and the NASL's San Diego Sockers, and it didn't take him long to make an impression. Sanchez's first game was an exhibition match against European powerhouse Dynamo Moscow, and he proceeded to score four goals in a 5-2 win, with three of them coming in a fourteen-minute span of the first half. Sanchez did much the same to NASL defenses over the next two seasons, scoring twenty-six goals in just thirty-two games, and leading the Sockers to the semifinals of the playoffs both times. Following his second visit in the summer of 1980, Sanchez's career reached escape velocity, playing for bigger clubs like

Atletico Madrid, as well as the granddaddy of them all, Real Madrid. It was in Spain where he won the La Liga scoring title, known as the "Pichichi," five times, as well as several league titles. Sanchez finished his career with the Dallas Burn of MLS, making him one of two players (Roy Wegerle is the other) to have played outdoors in both the NASL and MLS.

2. JULIO CESAR ROMERO

The Paraguayan joined the New York Cosmos in 1980, at which point he was already an established international, helping his country to the 1979 Copa America title. And Romero immediately lit up MLS, notching fourteen goals and nineteen assists, and helping the Cosmos to an NASL championship. After leading New York to another title in 1982, Romero left for Brazilian side Fluminense and achieved even greater renown. He was named South American player of the year in 1985, and helped Paraguay qualify for the 1986 World Cup, where he scored two goals in helping his team reach the second round.

3. ROBERTO CABAÑAS

The other half of the Cosmos' Paraguayan duo, Cabañas took a bit more time to settle in New York than his country-man Romero, but once he did, he ended up outlasting his teammate, and even won the league's MVP award in 1983. After the league folded, Cabañas moved on to Colombian club America de Cali, leading them to three consecutive appearances in the final of the Copa Libertadores, South America's continental club championship. And like Romero, he scored two goals for his country in the 1986 World Cup.

4. PETER BEARDSLEY

Beardsley is most often remembered for his exploits with

Liverpool's championship sides of the late '80s. But back in the earlier part of the decade, he was a player still trying to find his way, especially after being released by Newcastle United, the club he supported as a child. Enter the NASL's Vancouver Whitecaps, who along with English lower-tier side Carlisle United, gave Beardsley a chance to further hone his skills. Beardsley made the most of his time in North America, galvanizing the Whitecaps' attack, and leading them to the best regular season record in 1983. Following that campaign, Beardsley finally joined up with Newcastle, and went on to star for several clubs, as well as England's 1986 World Cup side that reached the quarterfinals.

5. TREVOR FRANCIS

By the time Francis arrived stateside, he was near his peak, having starred for Birmingham City as well as England's national team. His play with the Detroit Express was nothing short of exemplary, notching twenty-two goals in just nineteen games during his first season in the NASL. But in between his two seasons with Detroit, he achieved perhaps his greatest moment in the game, scoring on a diving header for Nottingham Forest to win the 1979 European Cup final (the precursor to today's Union of European Football Associations Champions League). After completing his second season with Detroit, one that saw him earn first-team All-Star honors, Francis went on to represent England at the 1982 World Cup.

6. PETER WITHE

While five players from England's 1966 World Cup-winning team plied their trade at one time or another in the NASL, Withe represented the complete other end of the spectrum—a player desperate to do anything to get his career headed in the right direction. Prior to arriving in the United States, Withe had been struggling to make an impact in English soccer, as witnessed by his paltry production of three goals in seventeen games during a two-year stint with Wolverhampton Wanderers. Fortunately for Withe, a spot in 1975 with the expansion Portland Timbers beckoned, and he proceeded to chalk up All-Star numbers, tallying seventeen goals in twenty-five matches. Such was Withe's prowess in the air that he was nicknamed "The Wizard of Nod" by the Portland fans. Withe's success in Portland proved to be just what he needed, as he subsequently enjoyed success with several top English sides. His best moment came in 1982 with Aston Villa, when he scored the only goal of that year's European Cup final.

7. BRUCE GROBBELAAR

With All-Star keeper Phil Parkes manning the nets, playing time was scarce for Grobbelaar during his first season with Vancouver in 1979. But the Zimbabwean, who was signed at a Whitecaps' scouting camp in South Africa, saw considerably more time the following season, and showed well enough to join English side Crewe Alexandria on loan. That move allowed him to catch the eye of Liverpool, for whom he starred during the rest of the '80s, winning thirteen championship medals.

8. GRAEME SOUNESS

Back before the mere sight of Souness's visage would cause opposition midfielders to melt, the Scot was struggling to crack the first team with Tottenham Hotspur, and in order to give him some seasoning, Spurs management sent the then nineteen-year-old over the pond to spend the summer of 1972 playing for Montreal Olympique. Souness made the most of his time in the NASL, earning first team All-Star honors despite toiling for a side that missed out on the playoffs. After returning to England, Spurs sold Souness to Middlesbrough, but Souness's best moments came later with the great Liverpool sides of the late '70s and early '80s, winning numerous trophies during his time with the Reds.

9. JAN VAN BEVEREN

Van Beveren was thirty-two years of age when the Ft. Lauderdale Strikers acquired him in 1980, but as a goalkeeper that meant that instead of being over-the-hill, he was at the peak of his incredible powers. For the next three years, van Beveren delivered countless world class saves behind a defense that made a cruise ship look nimble by comparison, and such artistry is the reason that many feel that had van Beveren not been ousted from Holland's national team at the behest of a certain Johan Cruyff, the Dutch might have a World Cup (or two) in their trophy cabinet.

10. MARK HATELEY

Hateley was another youngster who spent a summer in the United States to sharpen his game, following in Francis's footsteps by playing for the Detroit Express. Just eighteen-years-old at the time, Hateley was unable to build on Francis's considerable legacy, notching only two goals in nineteen matches. But the Englishman went on to have considerable success in his career, playing for such storied sides as A.C. Milan and Monaco, before enjoying his best years with the Scottish side Glasgow Rangers.

The Cradle of Coaches?

Okay, so about the only things the NASL was a cradle to were red ink and some dubious marketing strategies. But peruse the team rosters from those years, and more than a few famous coaches immediately catch the eye. And that doesn't even include the likes of Franz Beckenbauer and Johan Cruyff, who were destined for the hot seat the moment their playing days ended.

1. CESAR LUIS MENOTTI

It was the summer of 1967, the National Professional Soccer League, the precursor to the NASL, was in its inaugural (and only) season, and the league's New York entry, christened the Generals, slogged toward a mediocre 11-13-8 record. But unbeknownst to the players, there was a future World Cup-winning coach in their midst. At the time Menotti was a forward whose career was nearing its end. After scoring four goals that season, Menotti returned in 1968 for his second campaign (and the NASL's first) and upped his tally to five goals. After solitary campaigns with Brazilian sides Santos and Juventus, Menotti hung up his boots, but he was soon on the coaching fast track, leading unfancied Huracan to the Argentine championship. That led to his

eight-year tenure with Argentina's national team that included victory in the 1978 World Cup.

2. GUUS HIDDINK

Success has followed Hiddink at nearly every stop of his
coaching career, whether it was leading PSV Eindhoven to
European Cup glory in 1988, or taking the national teams
of South Korea and Australia to unprecedented heights. But
back in the late '70s and early '80s, Hiddink was a journeyman midfielder who plied his trade for such NASL sides as
the Washington Diplomats and the San Jose Earthquakes.
His experiences stateside gave him an appreciation for life
outside his native Holland, and helped pave the way for his
international coaching career.

3. JAVIER AGUIRRE

Unlike many of his countryman, the Mexican-born Aguirre
proved he could enjoy a successful playing career outside
of his homeland as well as inside it. Aguirre's travels took
him to Spain with Osasuna, but not before he spent a single
season with the Los Angeles Aztecs in 1980. That year he
played up top in leading the Aztecs to the semifinals of the
playoffs, falling to the eventual champions, the New York
Cosmos. As a coach, Aguirre enjoyed great success in
Mexico's Primera Division, and coached Mexico's national
team into the second round of the 2002 World Cup. Following that stint, Aguirre moved back to Spain, where he now
coaches Atletico Madrid.

4. DICK ADVOCAAT

Advocaat literally showed up on the doorstep of the Chicago
Sting in 1978, asking for a tryout. The Sting's general manager, Clive Toye, had every reason to send the Dutchman

on his way, but he decided to give Advocaat a chance, and was he ever glad he did, as Advocaat anchored Chicago's midfield for three productive seasons. Once his playing days were over, Advocaat became one of the most respected coaches in Holland, which meant he was criticized at every turn, by the country's legion of armchair coaches. One of Advocaat's first coaching stints was as an assistant to Rinus "The General" Michels, earning Advocaat the nickname "The Little General." Advocaat later took Holland to the 1994 World Cup, and he helped South Korea win their first ever World Cup match on foreign soil in 2006. Advocaat later excelled for several club sides, including Glasgow Rangers, and Zenit St. Petersburg in Russia, with whom he won the 2008 UEFA Cup.

5. GEORGE GRAHAM
The Scottish midfielder, a veteran of Arsenal's double-winning side of 1970–71, made his journey stateside in 1978, playing a solitary season for the California Surf. Graham might have stayed longer, but an ankle injury courtesy of the Surf's uneven artificial surface hastened his move back to Britain, and into management. Graham went on to revive an Arsenal side that had been underachieving for years, winning six trophies in eight seasons, including two league championships.

6. KLAUS TOPPMOELLER
The one-time German international was an injured shadow of his former self when he spent 1980 playing for the Dallas Tornado, with a gimpy knee limiting his effectiveness. Even though he managed seven goals and nine assists for Dallas, he soon returned to Germany and embarked on a successful coaching career. He took Bayer Leverkusen to the

2002 UEFA Champions League final, where they lost to Real Madrid, and the run, combined with a second place finish in the Bundesliga, saw Toppmoeller named Germany's Coach of the Year. Toppmoeller has bounced around a bit since then, including a stint with Georgia's national team.

7. HARRY REDKNAPP

Unlike many of his NASL contemporaries, Redknapp got a head start on his managerial career when he assumed a dual role of player/assistant coach during a four-year spell with the Seattle Sounders beginning in 1976. Redknapp made only twenty-four appearances during his time in the NASL, but the coaching baptism served him well, leading him to manage several EPL sides, including West Ham United, Southampton, and most notably, Portsmouth, with whom he won the 2008 FA Cup.

8. ROY EVANS

Evans spent nine years with the famed Liverpool sides of the '60s and '70s, but he could manage only eleven first-team appearances in a nine-year career. Yet in 1973, Evans joined the expansion Philadelphia Atoms, and his contributions in defense helped them win an improbable league title in their inaugural season. Evans soon returned to England, and joined Liverpool's coaching staff, rising through the ranks of the "Boot Room" to eventually be named their manager in 1994.

9. LEO CUELLAR

Cuellar's immense afro made him a long-time member of the World All-Hair XI, but he also enjoyed a stellar playing career that included an appearance at the 1978 World Cup as well as a stint as captain of Mexico's national team. He also spent six years in the NASL, first with the San Diego Sockers, and then with the San Jose/Golden Bay Earthquakes. When it comes to his coaching career, Cuellar has also been a bit unconventional. Instead of managing men's sides, Cuellar has spent most of the last decade as head coach of the Mexico women's national team, leading them to two Olympic berths as well as a spot in the 1999 World Cup.

10. JOMO SONO

South African apartheid prevented Sono from earning greater renown, but his six-year spell in the NASL, including a stint on the New York Cosmos' title-winning side of 1977, provided a platform for his coaching endeavors. Upon retirement in 1983, Sono returned to South Africa and started his own club, Jomo Cosmos. Sono also took time out from his club commitments to manage the South African national team on two occasions, leading them to the final of the 1998 African Cup of Nations, as well as coaching the side at the 2002 World Cup.

Yanks Abroad

For all the jibes about American soccer, there is no surer sign of its rise in stature than the increased flow of U.S. players to European leagues. In 2006, twenty-one American-born players made at least one first-team appearance in the major European leagues of England, Germany, Italy, France, and Spain with dozens more playing in the lower divisions of these countries and elsewhere. Here are those Yanks who made their mark in some of the world's toughest leagues.

1. CLAUDIO REYNA
The New Jersey-born Reyna holds a unique place in the annals of U.S.-born players. Not only has Reyna made more top-flight appearances in Europe than any other American outfield player, but he was also the first American to captain a European first division club when he donned the captain's armband for Wolfsburg in the German Bundesliga. Reyna also was named captain of Scottish club Rangers, and Manchester City of the English Premier League.

2. BRIAN MCBRIDE
McBride had loan stints in England with Preston North End and Everton before finally sticking with London-based club

Fulham F.C. in January 2004. Affectionately known by U.S. fans as "McHead" for his aerial prowess, McBride has scored at a steady clip for Fulham, tallying twenty-nine times in 126 games. His thirty-three goals while in England's top flight is a record for an American.

3. JOHN HARKES
One of America's trailblazers, Harkes was one of the first players to establish himself with a European club, making his mark with Sheffield Wednesday in the early '90s. He helped the Owls win the 1991 League Cup final against Manchester United, becoming the first American in over a century to capture a winner's medal in a senior competition. Harkes also spent time with English sides Derby County and West Ham United before finishing his career in the United States, mostly with D.C. United.

4. BRAD FRIEDEL
Friedel's career abroad got off to a rocky start, as he was thrice denied a work permit to play in England before securing a spot with Turkish side Galatasaray, where he helped them win the 1996 Turkish Cup. Following a brief stint in MLS, Friedel then struggled during a brief spell with Liverpool, before finding a home with English Premier League side Blackburn Rovers in 2000. Friedel has made over 250 appearances for Blackburn, and was named Man-of-the-Match in their 2002 League Cup triumph over Tottenham Hotspur. He was also named to the EPL's team of the season for 2003–04.

5. KASEY KELLER
Keller has enjoyed the longest European career of any American player, recording almost 500 appearances for a

smattering of clubs, including English clubs Millwall, Leicester City, Tottenham Hotspur, Southampton, and Fulham, as well as Spanish side Rayo Vallecano and Germany's Borussia Moenchengladbach. His stint with 'Gladbach saw him become the second American to captain a Bundesliga club.

6. PAUL CALIGIURI

Caligiuri was one of those American soccer pioneers with the arrows in his back to prove it. He created something of a sensation in 1987 when he signed for Bundesliga side Hamburg, but was never able to break into the first team. The California native eventually moved on to several second-tier German sides, and even spent time in East Germany with Hansa Rostock, helping them win the last league title contested in that country prior to German unification. After starring for the United States in the 1994 World Cup, Caligiuri finally realized a life-long dream, suiting up in the Bundesliga for Hamburg-based side St. Pauli.

7. ERIC WYNALDA

A performer whose talking made as many headlines as his play, Wynalda was the first American to make a first-team appearance for a Bundesliga club, joining Saarbrucken for the 1992–93 season. Wynalda's eight goals in the first half of the season seemed to position the club for a stay in the top flight, but the team was ultimately relegated to the second division. Wynalda eventually moved on to another Bundesliga side, Vfl Bochum, before returning to the United States to play in MLS.

8. STEVE CHERUNDOLO

Cherundolo is one of those rare players who has stayed with one club his entire professional career, having made over 200 appearances with German Bundesliga side Hannover 96 since joining the team in 1999. At 5-foot-6, 145 pounds, the slightly built Cherundolo found a home in the right side of Hannover's defense, keying their promotion from the second division in the 2001–02 season. The Portland, Oregon, native is also one of Hannover's two deputy captains.

9. JOHN O'BRIEN

Arguably the finest passer the United States has ever produced, O'Brien was that rare American player who made the move to Europe as a teenager, signing with famed Dutch club Ajax in 1994. O'Brien then rose through the ranks, signing his first professional contract in 1998, and went on to spend eight seasons in Holland. It was while he was with Ajax that O'Brien became the first American to play in the knockout stages of the UEFA Champions League.

10. BRENT GOULET

Only David Hasselhoff has played in more German stadiums than the North Dakota native, making Goulet the soccer version of *Bull Durham*'s Crash Davis. In a career that began in 1987 and lasted well over a decade, Goulet bounced around several lower-tier German sides, including Bonner SC, Tennis Borussia Berlin, Rot-Weiss Oberhausen, and Wuppertaler SV, before finally landing with third-division side Elversberg. But while Goulet the player may have been a journeyman at best, he managed to strike a blow for American soccer when in 2004 he was named Elversberg's head coach. It is believed that Goulet is the only American to have managed a European professional side.

Great Moments in Yanks Abroad History

While the evolution of American players can be charted by the lengthy European careers of some of its players, that progress can also be tracked by some signature moments that signaled the arrival of American soccer. These include some big games, memorable goals, as well as the sight of U.S. players hoisting trophies, including some of the most treasured in the history of the sport.

1. JULIAN STURGIS
While it's tempting to think of American soccer accomplishments as occurring only in the last thirty years, it was back in 1873 that Sturgis recorded a first for an American-born player. Born in Boston in 1848, Sturgis moved to England when he was just seven months old. By the early 1870s Sturgis was playing for amateur side Wanderers FC, and was part of the team that defeated Oxford 1-0 in the 1873 English FA Cup Final. It would take almost 120 years for an American to once again triumph in an English senior cup competition.

2. JOHN HARKES
Wembley Stadium in London is considered one of the

cathedrals of the game, and it was there that Harkes recorded a couple of memorable firsts for an American. When his Sheffield Wednesday side defeated Manchester United 2-1 in the 1991 League Cup final, Harkes became the first American to secure a winner's medal on Wembley's hallowed turf. When he scored the opening goal two years later in the final of the same competition against Arsenal, Harkes went into the record books again as the first American goalscorer in the final of a senior English cup competition. Away from Wembley, Harkes also earned Goal of the Year honors when his 40-yard blast against Derby in a 1991 League Cup match beat legendary goalkeeper Peter Shilton.

3. MIKE MASTERS

Harkes' tally was not the first scored by an American at Wembley, however. That distinction belongs to Mike Masters, who in 1992 scored for Colchester United in a tournament called the FA Vase Trophy, a competition for clubs outside the top four tiers of English soccer. Masters' goal propelled Colchester to a 3-1 triumph.

4. BRAD FRIEDEL

The Blackburn Rovers goalkeeper struck another blow for American players in 2003 when he was named to the English Premier League team of the season, an honor made all the more remarkable by his team's sixth place finish. Friedel was the first American to have been so honored in one of the elite leagues of Europe.

5. FULHAM VS. EVERTON

What was a non-descript midseason meeting in 2008 between Everton and Fulham FC went down in American soccer history when six Yanks—Fulham's Kasey Keller, Clint Dempsey, Brian McBride, Eddie Johnson, and Carlos Bocanegra; and Everton's Tim Howard—each took the field, as sure a sign as any of the increase in quality of American players. Fulham took the "Yanks Abroad Derby" 1-0 with McBride scoring the game-winning goal for the Cottagers.

6. DAMARCUS BEASLEY

The UEFA Champions League remains the Holy Grail of European soccer, and the Fort Wayne, Indiana, native played in the 2004–05 edition when his PSV Eindhoven squad reached the semifinals, falling to eventual champions AC Milan. Beasley later made history of a different sort when his goal for Rangers in the 2007–08 competition saw him become the first American to score goals for two different clubs in the Champions League.

7. JOVAN KIROVSKI

Kirovski first broke into European soccer with a Manchester United youth team that included David Beckham and Paul Scholes. But when Kirovski failed to secure a work permit in England, he was sold to German side Borussia Dortmund, where he entered the annals of Yanks Abroad lore. During a Champions League match against Sparta Prague on December 10, 1997, Kirovski's goal in Dortmund's 3-0 victory was the first by an American in the competition. Kirovski is also the only American to be a part of a UEFA Champions League winner, as Dortmund took the 1997 crown. And his substitute appearance in the 1997 World Club Cup (which pits the Champions League winner against its South American counterpart, the Copa Libertadores) made him the first American to appear in that competition as well.

8. KASEY KELLER

Keller has enjoyed one of the most durable careers in Europe for an American, but perhaps his best moment came during the 1997 League Cup, when Keller's unfancied Leicester City side defeated favorites Middlesbrough 1-0 in a replay to claim the only title of his professional career. Keller didn't have long to enjoy his triumph. He was on a plane back to the United States the next day to join up with his teammates on the national team, and he missed the celebration back in England.

9. STEVE TRITTSCHUH

When Trittschuh joined Sparta Prague for the 1990–91 season, he was an anomaly in more ways than one, playing not only in Europe but behind the iron curtain. His consistent play in defense helped Sparta win the Czechoslovakian league championship, a rare league title for an American. But where Trittschuh really made history was on December 10, 1990, when he took the field against Spartak Moscow, becoming the first American to play in the European Cup.

10. TIM HOWARD

The 2004 FA Cup Final wasn't the most dramatic of games, and with the famed Wembley undergoing renovations, the match took place at Cardiff's Millennium Stadium instead of its usual venue. But when Manchester United defeated Millwall 3-0 in the match, Howard was in the nets, becoming the second American, and the first in the modern era, to lift one of soccer's most prestigious trophies.

MLS Firsts

When Major League Soccer was born in 1995, most pundits assumed the role of Wilbur Wright instructing brother Orville that "it'll never fly." But having survived well into its second decade, it's worth looking back on MLS's 1996 inaugural season, and the moments that helped shape America's latest attempt at a top-flight league.

1. FIRST AMERICAN SIGNING: TAB RAMOS, NEW YORK METROSTARS

A key component to get the fledgling league off the ground was bringing home its top domestic players, and MLS achieved just that on January 3, 1995, when Ramos was acquired from Spanish side Real Betis.

The acquisition didn't end up being the happiest of homecomings, as the Uruguayan-born Ramos—one of the most gifted playmakers the United States has ever produced—went on to spend seven injury-plagued seasons with New York, scoring just nine goals in 121 matches.

2. FIRST FOREIGN SIGNING: JORGE CAMPOS, LOS ANGELES GALAXY

It was June 6, 1995, when Campos—he of the neon goalkeeper jerseys and jaw dropping forays into the attacking half—signed with MLS and was allocated to the Galaxy. The thinking of course was that Campos would attract fans from Southern California's massive Hispanic market, and while the team was well supported in its first season, the flirtation with MLS, for both Campos and Latin fans, proved brief.

The loyalties of immigrant fans continued to reside with clubs back in their country of birth, while Campos played only two seasons in L.A. before moving to Chicago in 1998. When he lost his starting job with the Fire to unheralded rookie Zach Thornton, Campos returned to Mexico to play with U.N.A.M. Pumas. ·

3. FIRST GOAL: ERIC WYNALDA, SAN JOSE CLASH

With time running down in the league's inaugural game between the San Jose Clash and D.C. United, the match appeared headed toward a scoreless tie, which would have necessitated a shootout; not exactly the kind of scoreline the league's bigwigs envisioned. But in the eighty-ninth minute, the Clash's Wynalda rode to the rescue. Taking a pass from Ben Iroha, Wynalda slipped the ball between the legs of United defender Jeff Agoos, before bending a shot around goalkeeper Jeff Causey. The strike gave the Clash a dramatic 1-0 victory and the league was off and running.

4. FIRST SHUTOUT: TOM LINER, SAN JOSE CLASH

At the other end of the field, Clash goalkeeper Tom Liner made another kind of history, keeping a clean sheet in the league's first-ever match. Liner could have set up a recliner in his penalty area, so seldom was his goal threatened. His subsequent MLS career proved unremarkable save for a memorable highlight in which a full-stretch dive saw his face connect with the goalpost. By 1998, Liner was out of MLS, but his name has been permanently etched in the lore of the league.

5. FIRST HAT TRICK: STEVE RAMMEL, D.C. UNITED
Not content with just dropping the first match in league history, United went on to lose their first four league contests. And by May 15, United were propping up the standings with a 1-6 record. But things began to turn around that day for head coach Bruce Arena's side when they pummeled the Columbus Crew 5-2, with Rammel netting the first hat trick in league history. Of course, it helped having the likes of Marco Etcheverrey running the offense, as the Bolivian delivered the first assist hat trick that day as well. Rammel's sole claim to that achievement was short lived, as New York's Giovanni Savarese equaled his feat just a day later.

6. FIRST RED CARD: JIM ST. ANDRE, NEW ENGLAND REVOLUTION
It wasn't anything as dramatic as a nasty challenge or fisticuffs, but the Revolution goalkeeper made it into the MLS record books anyway, when he was sent off for intentional handball outside the box late in New England's 3-2 loss to Tampa Bay on April 13, 1996. A veteran of various indoor and outdoor leagues in the United States, St. Andre's stay in MLS proved brief, lasting just a single season.

7. FIRST WINNING STREAK: LOS ANGELES GALAXY
No team put their stamp on the league during those first months quite like the Los Angeles Galaxy. With the likes of Eduardo Hurtado and Cobi Jones scoring at will, L.A. romped to twelve wins right out of the gate, and it wasn't until the Galaxy's ninth game against New England that

they were pushed to a shootout (MLS did not start counting ties until 1999). L.A.'s first loss finally came on June 30, 1996, when Colorado beat them 2-1 courtesy of goals by Roy Wegerle and Shaun Bartlett.

8. FIRST SCORING TITLE: ROY LASSITER, TAMPA BAY MUTINY

With the incomparable Carlos Valderrama controlling the offense, U.S. international Roy Lassiter enjoyed a dream season in 1996, scoring twenty-seven goals, an MLS record that still stands. Lassiter had previously plied his trade in the Costa Rican league with LD Alajuelense where he was named the top foreign player in 1995. But when MLS started in 1996, Lassiter came home and immediately clicked with Valderrama, leading the Mutiny to the best regular season record that season.

9. FIRST COACHING CASUALTY: EDDIE FIRMANI, NEW YORK METROSTARS

Just forty-four days after the team's first-ever game, Firmani became the first coach in league history to lose his job. Firmani had forged his coaching reputation in the old North American Soccer League leading the Tampa Bay Rowdies to the 1975 championship and taking the New York Cosmos to the title in 1977 and 1978. But despite fielding a team with the likes of U.S. internationals Ramos and Tony Meola, as well as Italian star Roberto Donadoni, the Metros stumbled to a 3-5 start, with two of those wins coming via shootout. With accusations mounting that Firmani was in over his head, he resigned his position, with current Manchester United assistant Carlos Querioz taking over.

10. **FIRST CHAMPIONSHIP: D.C. UNITED**

With a midseason record of 2-9, Arena was thinking of blowing up his side, but instead the United manager stayed the course. The result was a team that came together down the stretch, dispatching Eastern Conference regular season champions Tampa Bay in the conference finals.

The first-ever MLS Cup proved to be a microcosm of the United's season as well. L.A goals from Hurtado and Chris Armas staked the Galaxy to a 2-0 lead, but late strikes from Tony Sanneh and Shawn Medved took the game into overtime, where Eddie Pope's Golden Goal won it for the Black-and-Red.

Other MLS Milestones

The growth of MLS didn't begin and end with its first season. As the years passed, the league continued to shoehorn its way into the American sporting landscape, with developments both on and off the field accelerating its progress.

1. INTERNATIONAL COMPETITION

The best way for a league to gain credibility is for its teams to succeed in international competition, and no side did better in those early years than D.C. United. In 1998, the Black-and-Red became the first MLS side to claim the Confederation of North, Central American and Caribbean Association Football (CONCACAF) Champions Cup, when they defeated Mexican side Toluca 1-0. United followed up that triumph by winning the InterAmerican Cup, defeating Brazilian powerhouse Vasco de Gama 2-1 over two legs. Skeptics correctly pointed out that all of the games took place on U.S. soil, but it still proved to be a significant step toward respectability.

2. CREW STADIUM

Any improvement on the field would be wasted without

commensurate progress in the pocketbook, and the league took a quantum leap forward on May 15, 1999, with the opening of Crew Stadium, the country's first arena to be owned and operated specifically for a top-flight soccer team. A standing room only crowd of 24,471 packed the new venue to watch the Columbus Crew defeat New England 2-0. Importantly, as the season progressed the ancillary revenues from parking, concessions, and merchandise proved the concept that soccer-specific stadiums could work, giving MLS a financial blueprint for success. Since then, six more venues have been built along similar lines while ground has been broken on two more.

3. FIRST AMERICAN-BORN MVP
While the first years of MLS saw immense improvement in the play of domestic players, 1999 saw that process hit overdrive following the MVP season turned in by the Dallas Burn's Jason Kreis. The former fifth-round draft pick led the league that season in goals and points, and later became the first player in the league's history to break the 100-goal mark for his career.

4. SELLER'S MARKET
Anther sign of the league's progress has been the increased demand for its players. In 1999, goalkeeper Marcus Hahnemann was sold by MLS to EPL side Fulham for the wallet-busting fee of $90,000. Forward Joe-Max Moore signed with Everton a few months later for $50,000. Suffice it to say, the market for the league's players has gotten a tad warmer since then. In 2008, Jozy Altidore's services earned the league a minimum of $10 million when he was sold to Spanish club Villareal.

5. **CLINT MATHIS**

Leave it to Mathis to conjure up the single most dominating performance in MLS history. The former U.S. international, famous for his Mohawk at the 2002 World Cup as well as his mazy runs from midfield, lit up the Dallas Burn for five goals on August 26, 2000, while playing for the MetroStars. The Metros needed just about every one of them, too, as Mathis's penalty kick in the sixty-eighth minute put the visitors up 5-4 on their way to a 6-4 win.

6. **2002 WORLD CUP**

The United States made plenty of noise at the 2002 World Cup, reaching the quarterfinals for the first time since their semifinal run in 1930, and they had MLS to thank. Twelve of the roster's twenty-three players were playing with MLS clubs at the time of the tournament, while four others had also spent time in the league.

7. **IRON MAN**

As MLS heads into its thirteenth season, one player who has seen it all has been Steve Ralston. The veteran midfielder began his MLS career with the Tampa Bay Mutiny alongside the likes of Carlos Valderrama before moving on to New England, where he shared the stage with players such as Clint Dempsey and Taylor Twellman. Heading into the 2008 season, Ralston holds the mark for most appearances with 317, and has chalked up 121 assists, another league record.

8. **FIRST SHIRT SPONSOR**

In some parts of the world, the jerseys of some teams are plastered with so many sponsors that they bear a closer resemblance to racecars. The demand for such subliminal

advertising has been slower to reach MLS, although sponsorship on the back of team jerseys has been around since
the league began. But in 2006, Real Salt Lake broke the
mold, if not the bank, by becoming the first MLS side to
garner a sponsorship on the front of their jersey, with Utah-
based juice company XanGo getting the nod. Teams such
as Los Angeles, Chicago, and New York (whose nickname,
the Red Bulls isn't so subliminal) have since followed suit.

9. MUST-SEE TV
While MLS has had television deals throughout its history,
the landmark 2007 pact with Fox Sports, ESPN, and Spanish

The Los Angeles
Galaxy's David
Beckham looks up
field during an MLS
league match against
the Chicago Fire.
While Beckham's
first season in the
U.S. was marred by
injury, his signing
proved to be a major
milestone for MLS by
improving their
finances as well as
raising the league's
profile. *Tracy Allen/
isiphotos.com*

language network Telefutura broke new ground in that it was the first time that the league had received a rights fee in its brief history. Prior agreements saw MLS buying time for its broadcasts, but the new agreement signaled increased demand for the league's games.

10. **DAVID BECKHAM**

You didn't think you were going to make it through this book without a Beckham reference did you? The Englishman may have endured an injury-plagued first season in MLS, but there's no denying the impact that his signing had on the league's profile and finances. This was especially evident on August 18, 2007, when 66,237 fans crammed into Giants Stadium to see the New York Red Bulls prevail in a wild 5-4 win over the Los Angeles Galaxy, one that saw Beckham chip in with two assists in the losing effort.

Great Moments in MLS Playoff History

M ajor League Soccer hasn't been around for long, but in over a decade of existence the league has still managed to concoct its share of memorable moments. And nowhere is this more evident than in the postseason, where the pressure and bright lights have created enough drama and plot twists to fill a David Mamet script. Here are the matches that have most frayed the nerves of fans.

1. SAN JOSE EARTHQUAKES VS. LOS ANGELES GALAXY, 2003

The top-seeded Quakes entered the second leg of their aggregate goals series trailing the Galaxy 2-0, and the mantra of the day for San Jose was "don't concede another goal." So of course they conceded two goals from Carlos Ruiz and Alejandro Moreno in the first thirteen minutes, leaving them down 4-0 on aggregate. But San Jose then produced the most stunning rally in league history, scoring twice in the first half through Jeff Agoos and Landon Donovan, and equalizing in the second half through Jamil Walker and Chris Roner, the latter goal coming with just seconds remaining.

Out of substitutes in the overtime, and with Agoos

hobbled, a penalty kick shootout beckoned, but Donovan fed Rodrigo Faria in the box, and when his shot hit the back of the net, it completed the most unlikely of comebacks. It proved to be the only goal Faria ever scored for the club, but it was one that will long linger in the memory of San Jose fans.

2. DALLAS BURN VS. CHICAGO FIRE, 1999

A best-of-three game format was used for this playoff series and when the teams split the first two matches, a tense Game 3 loomed, one exacerbated by the fact that a nasty tackle from Chicago midfielder Dema Kovalenko had broken the leg of Dallas defender Brandon Pollard in Game 2. The match started off in the worst possible fashion for hosts Dallas, as Chicago scored twice in the game's first five minutes through Ante Razov and Jesse Marsch. But at that point the Fire seemed content to soak up Dallas's pressure, a move that would prove fatal. Chad Deering pulled a goal back in the fifty-fifth minute, and the home side equalized through a Jorge Rodriguez penalty kick with just six minutes remaining. Dallas struck for the game-winner just two minutes later, as Ariel Graziani pounded his shot off the underside of the bar and in for a dramatic victory.

3. D.C. UNITED VS. NEW ENGLAND REVOLUTION, 2004

When the two teams met on November 14 to decide who would move on to the MLS Cup final, little did they know that the match would be a classic. United took the lead three times, only to see the Revs respond each time, the final tally being Pat Noonan's equalizer with just five minutes to go. Both teams squandered clear chances in overtime, and for the first time in MLS history spot kicks would decide the winner.

The shootout proved as topsy-turvy as open play had been. United's Ben Olsen had his team's first attempt saved by Rev's goalkeeper Matt Reis, only to have New England's Steve Ralston slam his shot against the crossbar. D.C. goalkeeper Nick Rimando appeared to put United in the driver's seat when he stopped Jay Heaps' attempt in round four, but with the match on the line Reis saved Jaime Moreno's shot, and when Shalrie Joseph converted in round five, the Rev's were alive. Not for long, however. The sixth round saw Brian Carroll convert for United, while Rimando saved Clint Dempsey's attempt, and they were off to the MLS Cup final where they defeated Kansas City 3-2.

4. LOS ANGELES GALAXY, 2005

There was probably no more improbable run to a title than the Galaxy's success in 2005. L.A. had finished fourth in the Western Conference, a feat aided immensely by the fact that expansion sides Chivas USA and Real Salt Lake were in the same conference. But the Galaxy proved once and for all that a team's regular season record meant little when it came to the playoffs. With new acquisition Landon Donovan in electric form, the Galaxy dispatched bitter rivals (and top seed) San Jose 4-2 on aggregate in the first round, and then won on the road at Colorado 2-0 to make the MLS Cup final. The final against New England turned out to be a dour, defensive affair, but Pando Ramirez's volley in overtime saw the Galaxy prevail 1-0, and L.A.'s journey from bottom seed to champions was complete.

5. KANSAS CITY VS. SAN JOSE, 2004

One season removed from a championship, it was the fourth-seeded Earthquakes who attempted to pull the upset, and after a 2-0 win in the first leg of the aggregate goals series, all appeared well. But Kansas City produced a stirring fightback of their own. Wizards' goalkeeper Bo Oshoniyi produced a stunning save from a Landon Donovan drive to keep the Wizards within touching distance, and the home side then equalized through Khari Stevenson's goal and a Brian Ching own goal. With overtime looming, Jack Jewsbury then settled matters with a thumping drive from the top of the box, giving the Wizards a night to remember.

6. NEW YORK VS. D.C. UNITED, 1996

The inaugural playoff game in the league's first season proved to be one for the ages. Regulation time ended 2-2, and as ties were not allowed that year in MLS, the game would be decided by an NASL-style shootout. This edition went a fingernail devouring eleven rounds that included one attempt that resulted in a penalty when United goalkeeper Jeff Causey—who entered the match just for the shootout— hauled down New York's Roberto Donadoni, who converted his spot kick. Both goalkeepers were forced to shoot as well, with both Causey and New York's Tony Meola shooting wide. Finally, New York's Peter Vermes had a chance to win it in round 11, and when he did, howls of protest went up from United who claimed that Vermes had shot out of order. While it was confirmed that Vermes was slated to go in round 8, MLS ruled that no advantage had been gained, and the result stood.

United had the last laugh, however, coming back to win the series in three games, with Marco Etcheverry netting an eighty-ninth minute penalty in the series decider.

7. LOS ANGELES VS. NEW YORK, 2001

In 2000, the shootout was abandoned, and as a result play-off series were decided in a "first to five" format. Teams would get three points for a win and one point for a draw, and the first team to amass five points over three games would advance. But in the 2001 tilt between L.A. and New York, each team recorded a win, a loss, and a tie over the three matches, meaning that thirty minutes of extra time would be needed to decide the winner.

Making the situation even more tense was that a red card sustained by Los Angeles defender Danny Califf in Game 3 meant that L.A. would have to play short for the entire extra session. It seemed that only a bit of magic would allow Galaxy to survive, yet that's exactly what happened eight minutes into extra time. A Galaxy free kick from Mauricio Cienfuegos deflected off the head of New York's Mark Chung and past a stranded Tim Howard in the MetroStars net, and a miracle had been achieved.

8. KANSAS CITY VS. DALLAS, 1996

In what then ESPN broadcaster Keith Olbermann once dubbed, "a urologist's dream," it was the Wiz versus the Burn in this first round best-of-three matchup. Of course, in 1996 the shootout was alive and well, and in that year's memorable tilt it was used to decide the series—the only time that form of tiebreaker became a winner-take-all affair.

Much like the series, Game 3 featured mammoth momentum shifts, with Hugo Sanchez putting Dallas in front, only for Kansas to fight back through goals by Mark Chung and Digital Takawira. When Gerell Elliott equalized for Dallas, the shootout loomed. In that lottery Kansas City emerged victorious, with goalkeeper Garth Lagerwey earning hero status by saving three of the Burn's attempts.

9. CHICAGO VS. LOS ANGELES, 1998

If there was a team that most emulated the style of Brazil in those early days, it was 1998's edition of the Galaxy. The team set an MLS record for goals scored in a season that still stands, tallying a Ripley's-defying eighty-five times. The team's goal difference was a whopping plus-forty-one. Yet in the Western Conference finals, the Galaxy met the MLS equivalent of Italy, a Chicago Fire team with the defensive tenacity of a pit bull, and with enough attacking quality to keep teams honest. Coached by current U.S. national team coach Bob Bradley, the expansion Fire sprung a 1-0 upset in Los Angeles on a late Jesse Marsch goal. Keen to avoid a return trip to LA, Chicago won the second game in a shootout, and one of the great playoff upsets was complete.

10. NEW ENGLAND VS. NEW YORK, 2005

The Revolution's comeback against New York might have required fewer goals than San Jose's epic conquest of L.A. in 2003, but the warp speed at which they rallied in the second leg of their two-game series made that October 29 night one for the time capsule.

The Revs trailed from the first leg 1-0, and when New York's Youri Djorkaeff added to the MetroStars advantage with a fifty-ninth minute goal, a leviathan upset appeared in the making. But Jose Cancela pulled a goal back for the Revs just six minutes after coming on as a substitute, and when his corner kick was nodded home by Pat Noonan just five minutes later, New England were not only off life support, but gained a permanent hold of the game's momentum. Bermudan international Khano Smith completed the comeback in the eighty-third minute, when he fired home from the left side of the box, but there was still time for more heroics. New England's Shalrie Joseph cleared Djorkaeff's header off the line, and the Revs' miraculous comeback was in the books.

The Graduates

While Americans have been heading overseas in ever increasing numbers, the advent of MLS has seen that pace accelerate, with several of the league's players going on to perform in some of the best leagues in Europe.

1. DAMARCUS BEASLEY

After a four-year stint in MLS with the Chicago Fire, Beasley signed with Dutch side PSV Eindhoven, where his afore-mentioned exploits in the 2004–05 UEFA Champions League saw him score four times in twelve games. He also scored a memorable, last-minute equalizer in the Dutch Cup semifinal against Feyenoord that saw PSV eventually prevail on penalty kicks. Following a yearlong loan with EPL side Manchester City in 2006–07, the Scottish side Rangers signed Beasley.

2. CARLOS BOCANEGRA

Another product of the Chicago Fire, the one-time MLS Defender of the Year has been a regular performer in the back for London-based side Fulham in the English Premier League. Bocanegra has alternated between left back and the center of defense since his arrival in 2004, and he was

53

named captain of the side following Brian McBride's knee injury early in the 2007–08 season. All told, Bocanegra has tallied over one hundred appearances for the Cottagers.

3. TIM HOWARD
The latest in a long line of outstanding American keepers, Howard parlayed his six-season stint with the MetroStars into a big-money move to EPL giants Manchester United. Howard immediately was placed in the starting lineup and performed well initially. A series of high-profile mistakes then saw him condemned to the bench, but a transfer to fellow EPL side Everton saw Howard revive his career. His performance with Everton has made him the undisputed starting keeper for the U.S. national team.

4. CLINT DEMPSEY
After spending three seasons with the New England Revolution, Dempsey made no bones about his desire to head to Europe, and in January 2007 he joined the ever-growing American contingent at Fulham. While Dempsey struggled initially, his goal in a 1-0 win over Liverpool near the end of the season helped the Cottagers avoid relegation, and he continued his goal-scoring exploits during the 2007–08 season.

5. BOBBY CONVEY
When Convey joined D.C. United in 2000, at the time he was the youngest player ever signed by MLS. And such was his progress over the next four-plus seasons that he caught the eye of English scouts, finally signing for Reading in 2004. It took his entire first season in England to settle, but during the 2005–06 campaign, Convey was an ever-present force in the Reading lineup, helping them win promotion to the EPL.

6. **MARCUS HAHNEMANN**

Hahnemann was present for some of the early days of MLS, toiling for the Colorado Rapids from 1997 until midway through the 1999 campaign. At that point, he joined Fulham, and his career went down one of those rat holes that so often beckon to Americans overseas. But in 2002, Hahnemann finally escaped Fulham for second-tier side Reading, and along with Convey helped his team gain promotion to the EPL.

7. **MICHAEL BRADLEY**

When Bradley first broke in with the MetroStars in 2004, many assumed that his place on the team was due entirely to the presence of his father Bob, who at the time was the MetroStars head coach. But in 2006, the younger Bradley moved on to Dutch side Heerenveen, and his performances in a central midfield role have seen him pop up for numerous goals. In fact his nineteen strikes in all competitions during the 2007–08 campaign set a record for most goals in a single season by an American. Bradley has since moved on to German side Borussia Mönchengladbach.

8. **EDDIE LEWIS**

A four-year stint with the San Jose Clash saw Lewis earn Best XI honors in his final season. That proved to be the catalyst for his move to England, although it initially appeared as though Lewis wouldn't see a scintilla of playing time. Manager Paul Bracewell brought Lewis to Fulham, but Bracewell's firing and the subsequent hiring of Frenchman Jean Tigana as manager saw Lewis placed in purgatory. But a transfer to Preston North End saw Lewis finally earn some significant playing time, and he then went on to play with Leeds United before returning to the EPL with Derby County.

9. **GREG VANNEY**

While most American players have traveled to Britain and Germany in their search for European glory, Vanney took the road less traveled, landing on the island of Corsica with French first division side Bastia. This followed a six-season spell with the Los Angeles Galaxy, one that saw the side annually contend for honors, but ultimately fall short, losing three MLS Cup finals.

10. **TONY SANNEH**

After winning two MLS titles with D.C. United, the "Big Cat" took his game to Germany in 1998 with Bundesliga side Hertha Berlin, becoming one of the first American MLS products to make a move overseas. Sanneh went on to play three seasons with Hertha before spending another three campaigns with fellow top-flight side Nuremberg. Injuries hampered Sanneh's time in Germany, but he still managed over eighty Bundesliga appearances before returning to MLS in 2004.

Top MLS Imports

Of the numerous arrows that have been slung MLS's way during its existence, one has been its reputation as a haven for foreign has-beens, content to pick up a pay-check and nothing else. And as you'll see in a later chapter, there certainly have been plenty of imports who matched that description.

But there have also been those foreigners who have more than punched their weight, guys who not only brought their A-game to MLS stadiums throughout the country, but who were committed to the league for the long haul.

1. JAIME MORENO, D.C. UNITED AND METROSTARS

Moreno was a huge influence behind United's first three championships, and after recovering from a back injury that nearly ended his career, he rediscovered his best form in leading the Black-and-Red to their fourth title in 2004. A master on the ball with his vision, passing, and change of pace, Moreno is the one guy to whom you can't afford to give any room. A three-time Best XI selection, Moreno's 112 goals heading into the 2008 season are tops all-time in MLS.

D.C. United forward Jaime Moreno looks toward a goal in a 2007 MLS match between D.C. United and the Los Angeles Galaxy. Entering the 2008 season, Moreno's 112 goals are the most in league history. *Jose L. Argueta/ isiphotos.com*

2. PETER NOWAK, CHICAGO FIRE

Nowak was perhaps the best two-way player ever to grace MLS. While the Pole was amazingly quick with the ball at his feet, it was his attitude for which he is best remembered. Nowak would have run over a kitten to get to the ball, putting to rest any fears fans had that he was here for a vacation. A three-time Best XI selection, Nowak's tenacity and leadership were what head coach Bob Bradley built his side around. He later brought those same qualities as a coach, leading D.C. United to the 2004 championship before taking up an assistant's role with the U.S. national team.

3. **MARCO ETCHEVERRY, D.C. UNITED**

So bad was Etcheverry at the start of 1996, that head coach Bruce Arena nearly traded him away. It turned out to be the best move he didn't make, as "El Diablo" was one of the driving forces behind United's first three championships, with his game-altering free kicks and incredible vision. Several foreign clubs tried to sign the Bolivian, but he stayed in MLS, much to the delight of the United faithful.

4. **MAURICIO CIENFUEGOS, LOS ANGELES GALAXY**

When the diminutive Salvadoran was allocated to the Galaxy for the inaugural MLS season in 1996, the Los Angeles midfield was set for the next eight years. Cienfuegos was a guy who knew how to dictate the pace of a game, and while his numbers weren't always dazzling, the fact that the Galaxy were annual contenders for MLS Cup throughout his time in L.A. spoke volumes as to his influence.

5. **CARLOS VALDERRAMA, TAMPA BAY MUTINY, MIAMI FUSION, COLORADO RAPIDS**

He didn't play a lick of defense. But so what? When "El Pibe" had the ball at his feet, something magical often happened. Think of all the forwards that had career years when playing with the Columbian: Roy Lassiter, Mamadou Diallo, Musa Shannon (Who? Exactly!) Valderrama's mark of 114 regular season assists ranks second in MLS history.

6. **CARLOS RUIZ, LOS ANGELES GALAXY, F.C. DALLAS, AND TORONTO F.C.**

"The Little Fish" has been tormenting defenses with his lethal finishing—and theatrics—ever since he set foot in MLS back in 2002. It was during that season that Ruiz was the league MVP, and his overtime winner gave the Galaxy their lone MLS championship.

Off-field controversies—like his penchant for missing practice—have somewhat tainted his time in MLS. But there can be no doubting the quality of his play while on the field.

7. LUBOS KUBIK, CHICAGO FIRE AND DALLAS BURN

A member of Chicago's famed "Eastern Bloc," Kubik helped the Fire to the double in their inaugural season. In addition to his towering presence in defense, Kubik was also deadly from free kicks and a calming influence with the ball at his feet. The Czech finished his MLS adventure in Dallas, where a knee injury put an end to his career.

8. RYAN NELSEN, D.C. UNITED

Prior to the 2004 playoffs, an MLS head coach was asked to pick the MLS Cup winner other than his own team. The coach responded "D.C. United, if Nelsen stays healthy." As it turned out, those words proved prophetic. Nelsen's gritty play in the back, as well as his leadership, allowed United to become MLS's first four-time champions. That Nelsen now plies his trade in the EPL for Blackburn Rovers speaks to the quality of the Kiwi's overall game.

9. DWAYNE DE ROSARIO, SAN JOSE EARTHQUAKES AND HOUSTON DYNAMO

When De Rosario first broke into MLS, he established himself as a forward with a flair for the dramatic (witness his golden goal in the 2001 MLS Cup final) as well as being a ball hog. But a move to the center of midfield in 2005 saw the Canadian become one of the most dynamic players in MLS, earning two Best XI honors as well as twice winning the league's Goal of the Year award. He's also been part of four championship teams, twice winning the MLS Cup's MVP award.

10. **RONALD CERRITOS, SAN JOSE EARTHQUAKES, DALLAS BURN, D.C. UNITED**

The inclusion of Cerritos is bound to make fans in Washington and Dallas choke on their morning coffee. But the Salvadoran was one of the league's best strikers in the late '90s, despite toiling for some horrible San Jose teams. The leading scorer on the Quakes' championship side of 2001, Cerritos enjoyed something of a renaissance in his second go-round with San Jose, where he set up goals in addition to scoring them.

Foreign Flops in MLS

They came. They saw. They stunk. And some didn't even stick around long enough to show just how bad they were on the field. The topic of course is the worst foreign signings ever to grace Major League Soccer. MLS has often been derided as an over-the-hill league, and these players did all they could to maintain that reputation.

1. LOTHAR MATTHÄUS, NEW YORK METROSTARS
The German international still had plenty left in the tank when he joined the Metros in 2000. Matthäus was just coming off a season in which he led German side Bayern Munich to a domestic league title and played in the 1999 UEFA Champions League final. But his single season in the United States was characterized by indifference, especially when he was spotted recuperating from a back injury in that noted rehab facility known as St. Tropez.

2. GILLES GRIMANDI, COLORADO RAPIDS
In January 2003, head coach Tim Hankinson thought that signing the former Arsenal player was the answer to his midfield troubles. Those plans blew up in Hankinson's face when Grimandi arrived for training camp, took a look around the

place, and bolted back to Europe. Among the reasons that Grimandi cited were isolation from his family, as well as some anti-French sentiment on the part of fans (the U.S. invasion of Iraq, which France opposed, had just started). The defection cost the Rapids little monetarily, but there was no getting back the time spent wooing the want-away Frenchman.

3. BRANCO, NEW YORK METROSTARS

The Brazilian World-Cup winner's time in MLS was brief, but memorable, that is unless you are a MetroStars fan. His stat line read more like a rap sheet: eleven games, one goal, and three red cards, one of which was for spitting in an opponent's face and then throwing the ball at the referee. No sooner had the 1997 season ended than Branco was released.

4. KHODADAD AZIZI, SAN JOSE EARTHQUAKES

When the 1996 Asian Player of the Year arrived in San Jose in 2000, the Quakes thought they were receiving a creative dynamo who would kick-start their attack. A quick conversation with his previous employers FC Cologne would have revealed they were getting a temperamental player with poor training habits and a penchant for lashing out at his coaches. Alas, Azizi lived up to the latter characterization. When he wasn't losing the ball, he was feuding with referees, and he quickly wore out his welcome in San Jose. He played only a single forgettable season with the Earthquakes, tallying a measly three goals, and four assists in 20 games. His most memorable moment? A three-game suspension for attempting to slug an opponent and hitting the referee instead.

5. DANIEL AMOKACHI, COLORADO RAPIDS

The Nigerian's experience in MLS was a carbon copy of

Grimandi's, except it was Colorado who this time pulled the plug. The World Cup veteran showed up at training camp in 2002 woefully out of shape, and rather than wait for him to get fit, the Rapids waived Amokachi five days before the start of the season.

6. DENILSON, FC DALLAS

Dallas was cruising along during the 2007 season and was in first place in the Western Conference as late as August, when, like New York, it signed another Brazilian World Cup–winner who did more harm than good. When Denilson came on board later that month, the team went into an immediate tailspin, with the Brazilian's ball hogging doing little to endear himself to his teammates. Denilson's contribution consisted of one penalty kick goal, and no assists. He was waived at the end of the season.

7. LUIS HERNANDEZ, LOS ANGELES GALAXY

Before David Beckham was brought over to help spur MLS's growth, Hernandez was imported in 2000 to do the same thing, the idea being to tap into L.A.'s vast Hispanic market. Yet what resulted became known as "the circus effect." Fans came to see him once, and didn't bother coming back. Hernandez's attitude toward the league didn't help. He once failed to show up for a CONCACAF Champions Cup match, and his insistence that he be loaned out to teams in Mexico, even while MLS was in season, spoke volumes about his lack of commitment to the league.

8. SERGIO GALVAN REY, NEW YORK METROSTARS

It's been said that the league's New York entrant has been cursed, and given the saga of Rey, there might be some truth to that. The "King of Goals" arrived in the United States fresh from leading Colombian side Once Caldas to the 2003 league championship, and his total of 171 goals in ten years with the club had MetroStars fans salivating. But soon, they were crying, as Rey scored just two goals in twenty matches during the 2004 campaign. His fortunes improved somewhat during the following season, when he tallied seven times, but the Metros were eager to unload his hefty salary, and he was sold to Colombian side Atletico Nacional. Of course, no sooner had he returned to South America than the goals started flowing again.

9. CHRIS WOODS, COLORADO RAPIDS

Woods arrived in the United States with an impeccable goalkeeping pedigree, having played for such sides as Rangers, Sheffield Wednesday, as well as earning forty-three appearances with England's national team. But in a country where quality goalkeepers are as plentiful as shopping malls, Woods was deemed an expensive luxury, and lasted just one forgettable season in MLS, one that saw him rank near the bottom of the league's goalkeepers.

10. SEBASTIAN ROZENTAL, COLUMBUS CREW

The Crew had high hopes that the Chilean would be the creative force to revitalize the team's attack. What they got instead was a player with dodgy knees who reported to training camp so out of shape that it took him half the season to crack the Crew's starting lineup on a consistent basis. When he did, he had little impact, notching just three goals and one assist. Rozental was gone after just one season.

A League of Their Own

It may have only lasted three years, but the WUSA did succeed in providing female players with the greatest platform at club level the women's game has ever seen. And while efforts continue to revive a top-flight women's league in the United States, it's worth remembering that the WUSA did provide its fans with some memorable moments.

1. FIRST (AND SECOND) DRAFT

While the U.S. women's national team players were evenly dispersed among the WUSA's eight teams, a different fate awaited the league's contingent of foreign, college, and lesser known domestic players. A foreign allocation draft took place to distribute eight pairs of players, with Norwegian goalkeeper Bente Nordby and her international teammate, midfielder Hege Riise, joining the Carolina franchise. The selection proved to be a mixed bag. Nordby played only one season in the WUSA, but the choice of Riise laid the foundation for the Carolina's championship team of 2002.

Six weeks later, another draft was held to stock the remaining roster spots, and Chinese star Sun Wen was the first player chosen by Atlanta. Often thought to have been the equal of Mia Hamm, Sun was hobbled by age and injury during her WUSA tenure. She scored just five goals over two seasons, although she tallied twice more in the 2001 playoffs.

2. FIRST GOAL

April 14, 2001, was a landmark day in women's sports, as the WUSA kicked off its inaugural season with the Washington Freedom taking on the Bay Area CyberRays in front of 34,178 fans. The game was billed as a matchup between Washington's Mia Hamm and the Bay Area's Brandi Chastain, and sure enough, the two international stars were involved in the game's critical moment, when in the seventieth minute, Chastain was adjudged to have hauled Hamm down in the box. But in a league that was largely populated by Americans, it was left to a Brazilian named Pretinha to enter her name in the history books when her penalty kick beat Bay Area goalkeeper LaKeysia Beene for the game's only goal.

3. FIRST SHUTOUT

As much as the assembled crowd was there to cheer on Mia and Brandi, the Player of the Game in that first match might well have been Washington goalkeeper Siri Mullinix. The Freedom netminder made eight saves, including a sprawling stop from the Bay Area's Sissi in the sixty-sixth minute. Twenty-four odd minutes later, Mullinix had recorded the first clean sheet in league history.

4. FIRST HAT TRICK

One interesting development during the WUSA's first season was the way several of the league's marquee players struggled to dominate the way they had at international level. Hamm, hobbled by a troublesome knee, didn't even crack the top ten in scoring that year, but one player who settled in immediately was New York's Tiffeny Millbrett. The Portland, Oregon, native not only led the league in scoring that year, but she also notched the first hat trick in league history on June 22, 2001, during the Power's 3-1 win over Boston. Millbrett also took MVP honors at season's end.

5. FIRST ASSIST HAT TRICK
While Chastain walked off the field on the short end of the league's first match, things couldn't have been more different than when the two teams met again three months later. Hamm scored twice, but the CyberRays emerged with a 3-2 win, with Chastain recording the first assist hat trick in league history.

6. FIRST RED CARD
Any concerns that WUSA players might ease up on their international teammates evaporated on June 17, 2001, in a match between the Atlanta Beat and the San Diego Spirit. In the ninetieth minute of what would be a 3-2 Atlanta win, Beat forward Cindy Parlow swung an elbow after getting pushed from behind by San Diego's Julie Foudy. The swing connected with Foudy's jaw, momentarily silencing "Loudy" Foudy, and earning Parlow the first red card in league history.

7. FIRST UNBEATEN STREAK
Fastest out of the gate in 2001 was the Atlanta Beat, whose early domination was punctuated by an unbeaten streak over their first six games that nearly lasted into June. The key to Atlanta's quick start was the two-pronged attack of Parlow and Canadian international forward Charmaine Hooper.

8. FIRST FIRING

Unlike their brethren in MLS, it took the WUSA a bit longer to fire a coach, with San Diego's Carlos Juarez earning that dubious distinction in the middle of the 2002 season. Kevin Crow, the team's general manager, took over on an interim basis for the rest of the year, but there was no change in the Spirit's results. Just like in 2001, they failed to reach the playoffs.

9. BEST SINGLE-GAME PERFORMANCE

While Millbrett notched the first hat trick in league history, Chinese international Liu Ailing exceeded her exploits on August 6, 2001. During Philadelphia's 5-1 demolition of the Carolina Courage, Liu scored three goals and added an assist, a feat that wasn't equaled until almost two years later by both Atlanta's Maribel Dominguez and Carolina's Daniele Fotopoulos.

10. FIRST CHAMPION

While the first game in league history was a defensive struggle, the first championship match between Atlanta and the Bay Area contained plenty of offensive fireworks that pushed the drama meter into the red zone. The match was tied 2-2 late, when Atlanta's Sun Wen scored the apparent game-winner in the eighty-fourth minute. But the CyberRays' Tisha Venturini equalized just two minutes later, sending the match into overtime, and then penalty kicks. For a while it looked like the two heroes of the 1999 Women's World Cup final—Atlanta goalkeeper Brianna Scurry and Bay Area defender Brandi Chastain—would square off. But Bay Area goalkeeper LaKeysia Beene settled matters instead, saving Sun's attempt, and with Chastain waiting in the wings, the Bay Area's Julie Murray netted the winning penalty for a 4-2 shootout victory.

World Cup Qualifying Heartbreak

When the World Cup finals commence every four years, all eyes are on the thirty-two countries that have made it to soccer's biggest stage. Forgotten is the fact that over 170 other countries have already been eliminated from a qualification process, making Jason's trip on the Argo look like a Sunday stroll. Along the way, more than a few teams have had qualification in their sights only to fall at the last second, taking up permanent residence in the World Cup's Heartbreak Hotel.

1. CAMEROON (2006)

The Indomitable Lions appeared set to qualify for their sixth finals when they defeated the Ivory Coast 3-2 in their penultimate match. That put them a point ahead of the Ivorians in the standings, meaning they could guarantee qualification with a win at home over Egypt. An early goal from Rudolph Duala put Cameroon ahead, but Egypt's Mohammed Shawky equalized late in the match and with the Ivory Coast winning their match over Sudan, Cameroon had no choice but to launch an all-out assault on the Egyptian goal.

Cameroon's prayers appeared to be answered five minutes into stoppage time when they were awarded a penalty, at which point the Lions turned into Lambs, as a colossal case of stage fright ensued. No one but Pierre Wome was willing to take the spot kick, and to the home crowd's shock, Wome blasted his attempt against the post, leaving Cameroon out of the Cup. Afterwards, the courage of star striker Samuel Eto'o underwent a remarkable recovery, claiming that he wanted to take the penalty, but was pushed aside by Wome. Wome insisted otherwise.

2. TRINIDAD & TOBAGO (1990)
The Caribbean nation's task was simple. All they had to do was gain at least a draw at home against the United States, and they would be heading to the World Cup finals for the first time. The result was thought to be a foregone conclusion. The United States had not won a road match in nearly two years, and a national holiday was declared in the island nation on the day of the match. Yet in a heartrending turn of events, a looping shot from U.S. defender Paul Caligiuri found the back of the net in the thirty-fifth minute, and T&T were unable to find a breakthrough, leaving their World Cup dreams in tatters.

3. AUSTRALIA (1998)
Faced with a two-legged playoff against Iran, the Socceroos were in good shape when they tied the first leg 1-1 in Tehran. Things looked even better when Australia went up 2-0 on goals by Harry Kewell and Aurelio Vidmar. Yet when Australian serial prankster Peter Hore, in a Steve Bartman moment, ran onto the field and cut the net following Vidmar's goal, a delay ensued. In that time, the Iranians hatched a brilliant plan that consisted of "get the ball to Khodadad Azizi as much as possible." So noted, Azizi fed Karim Bagheri for a goal in the seventy-fifth minute, and he scored the equalizer himself four minutes later. When the final whistle

blew, the score was 3-3 on aggregate, but Iran advanced by virtue of having scored more away goals. Australia thus earned the dubious distinction of having failed to qualify despite not losing a single game.

4. FRANCE (1994)

The French collapsed quicker than the Maginot line during qualification for the 1994 tournament. With two home games remaining, all France had to do was win one of them to secure a spot in the finals. A stunning 3-2 defeat to Israel cranked up the pressure, but a draw in their last game against Bulgaria would still be enough. With the score 1-1 late in the match, that appeared to be exactly what the French would get. But with time winding down and the French in possession, midfielder David Ginola opted to cross the ball instead of keeping it, and Bulgaria promptly went down the field and scored on practically the last kick of the game on a goal by Emil Kostadinov.

The repercussions were more than just a few Gallic shrugs. Head coach Gerard Houllier resigned, and Ginola was never again chosen for a major tournament.

5. SPAIN (1954)

The '50s are often referred to as "a simpler time," and that went for World Cup qualifying as well. In Spain's case, a simple home-and-away series with Turkey was all that stood in their way. Yet when both matches finished 2-2, the play-off was decided by that most athletic of endeavors, drawing lots. Spain drew the proverbial short straw and became the first country eliminated via a tiebreaker.

6. TUNISIA (TOO MANY TIMES TO COUNT)

For all of the talk about the soccer war between El Salvador and Honduras, it's amazing that one didn't break out between Tunisia and fellow North Africans, Morocco. In a 1961 playoff, three games left the teams level on goals. That meant the dreaded lots were used again, and Morocco advanced. The same thing happened in qualifying for the 1968 Olympics, so by the time the 1970 qualifiers rolled around, the Tunisians were more paranoid than Fox Mulder on crystal meth. Sure enough, three games decided nothing, except this time the tiebreaker of choice was a coin flip. You didn't really expect it to end any other way did you? Tunisia lost, with their federation actually sending film to FIFA contending the coin flip was rigged. Needless to say, their protests were turned down.

7. **MOROCCO (1978)**
Eight years later, the Tunisians finally got their revenge. You know the script by now: Two games; even on goals; on to the tiebreak. Except by this time FIFA had wised up and decided a slightly more merciful form of Russian roulette should be used. And so the penalty kick shootout was born, at least in a World Cup qualifying sense. This time, the Tunisians finally came out on top, making Morocco the first team to ever be eliminated from qualifying via penalties.

8. **URUGUAY (2006)**
Having defeated Australia in a playoff for the 2002 World Cup, the two adversaries met again with a spot in the 2006 tournament on the line. Each side won 1-0 on home soil, and after extra-time was goalless, penalties beckoned. While Morocco was the first to feel penalty pain in a World Cup qualifier, it would be Uruguay who would be the first to lose a shootout with a direct spot in the finals at stake. Dario Rodriguez and Marcelo Zalayeta wore the goat horns for

Uruguay when Australian keeper Mark Schwarzer saved both of their penalties.

9. JAPAN (1994)

Asian qualifying for the 1994 edition was a six-team tournament held in Qatar, with the top two teams going through. By the time the final day arrived, five nations still had a shot at qualifying. Japan was one of the teams in control of their own destiny, and when Masashi Nakayama scored in the eightieth minute to put them 2-1 up on Iraq, a trip to the United States was in their sights. But Iraq responded with a stoppage-time equalizer from Jaffar Omran Salman, breaking Japanese hearts and delaying their first trip to the finals by another four years.

10. BELGIUM (1974)

The Belgians have one of the more impressive World Cup pedigrees, having qualified for the finals six times, and even reaching the semifinals in 1986. Yet during qualification for the 1974 tournament, they achieved some rather dubious distinctions. Not only did they go unbeaten, winning four matches and drawing twice, but they also did not concede a goal. Yet it wasn't good enough to qualify, as archrivals Holland, led by Johan Cruyff, beat them based on superior goal difference of +22 compared to Belgium's +12.

The final match in Amsterdam between the two sides was one that still raises the hackles of Belgium fans. Forward Gert Verhayen appeared to have won the game on a free kick with just seconds remaining. But the referee, one Kharakov from Russia, disallowed the goal for offside, even though television replays showed otherwise.

Great Players Who Never Played in a World Cup

The World Cup represents the pinnacle of just about any player's career. Many a performer's reputation has been enhanced when the entire world was watching. Yet not every player has been able to grace the game's biggest stage. Whether it was down to injury, weak national teams, or political turmoil, these great players never played in a World Cup finals.

1. ALFREDO DI STEFANO (ARGENTINA AND SPAIN)

Considered the greatest player of his generation, the Real Madrid legend is best known for helping the team win five consecutive European Cups (the forerunner to the UEFA Champions League) in the late '50s and early '60s, and scoring in each of those finals. Unfortunately, di Stefano's international career was plagued by a colossal case of bad timing. Argentina, his country of birth, declined to participate in both the 1950 and 1954 World Cups, denying di Stefano the opportunity to play.

Upon acquiring Spanish citizenship in 1956, di Stefano threw his international lot in with his adopted country, but they failed to qualify in 1958. "The Blonde Arrow" had a last chance 1962, and while he succeeded in helping Spain reach the finals in Chile, a pulled thigh muscle just prior to the tournament prevented di Stefano from playing, and his shot at World Cup glory was gone.

2. ALBERTO PEDRO SPENCER (ECUADOR)

"The Magic Head" remains a legend in South American soccer circles, starring for Uruguayan club Penarol in the '60s, where he led the side to eight league championships, three Copa Libertadores crowns, and two Intercontinental Club Cup titles. His total of fifty-four career goals in the Copa Libertadores remains a record, and the speed and power with which he played were immense.

Yet Spencer's international career remains shrouded in mystery. He switched allegiances between Uruguay and home country Ecuador several times, despite never being an official citizen of Uruguay. And since Ecuador couldn't produce a team on par with Spencer's undeniable skill, "La Cabeza Magica" never played in a World Cup. In all, Spencer appeared just eleven times for Ecuador and just four times for Uruguay, a paltry sum for a player regarded as one of South America's all-time greats.

3. GEORGE BEST (NORTHERN IRELAND)

Such was the reverence for Best in his home country, that at his funeral in 2005 a banner read "Maradona good; Pelé better; George Best." And as one of the first soccer stars of the television age, Best's amazing close control and on-the-ball trickery captivated fans everywhere and led Manchester United to two league titles and a European Cup crown in 1968.

Yet Best never duplicated such feats for Northern Ireland in World Cup qualifying. "The Belfast Boy" often backed out of international matches due to injury, and his love of the night life, as well as the overall lack of quality in the Northern Irish sides in the '60s and '70s didn't help. Northern Ireland finally qualified for the 1982 finals in Spain. But manager Billy Bingham opted to leave the country's most famous player at home, because at age thirty-six, Best's considerable skills had been blunted by his decades-long battle with alcoholism.

4. ABEDI PELE (GHANA)

Not to be confused with that "other" Pelé, the Ghanaian version was one of the first African players to make an impact on the European club scene. His incisive midfield displays for the Marseille teams of the early '90s helped them reach two European Cup finals, including a victory in the 1993 edition. Pele was also named African Player of the Year on numerous occasions by various outlets.

Yet when it came to World Cup qualifying, Pele and his talented "Black Stars" endured a puzzling run of underachievement. Ghana was often found among the favorites for the African Cup of Nations, winning the event in 1982 and making the final in 1992. But internal squabbling often undermined the team's best efforts. At issue was a dispute between Pele and striker Anthony Yeboah, with their tribal allegiances alleged to be at the root of their disagreement. It was not until 2006, long after Pele's retirement, that "The Brazil of Africa" finally reached the World Cup finals.

5. GEORGE WEAH (LIBERIA)

Weah enjoyed a phenomenal club career, playing for such well-known teams as Monaco, Paris St. Germain, Chelsea, and Marseille. But it was with Italian side AC Milan that Weah made his mark, leading the Rossoneri to the Serie A title in both 1996 and 1999. And in 1995, Weah was named

FIFA World Player of the Year. He remains the only African player ever to receive that honor.

At international level, however, Weah was never able to take Liberia to a World Cup, although not for lack of trying. The country was wracked by civil war for much of his career, yet Weah almost single-handedly kept Liberia's World Cup dream alive ahead of the 2002 edition, acting as player, coach, and chief financial backer. Alas, Liberia was edged out on the final day of qualifying by Nigeria, denying Weah his World Cup dream.

6. ERIC CANTONA (FRANCE)

The Frenchman won nearly everything at Manchester United, and it was his improvisation and creativity in attack that drove the Red Devils to four Premier League titles and two FA Cups in the '90s. Yet the self-destruct button that Cantona pressed periodically was at the heart of his World Cup absence. Manager Henri Michel banned Cantona from the French national team in 1988 after the mercurial midfielder insulted him in a post-match interview. With Cantona back in the side following Michel's ouster, France then failed to qualify for the 1994 tournament when they lost 2-1 at home to Bulgaria on a last-minute goal by Emil Kostadinov.

The 1998 World Cup, to be hosted by France, loomed as Cantona's last chance, but his suspension in 1995 for kicking a spectator saw him banned from international soccer for eight months. In that time, French manager Aime Jacquet rebuilt the side around a certain Zinedine Zidane, and Cantona was cast adrift. His retirement in 1997 at just thirty years of age sealed his international fate.

7. RYAN GIGGS (WALES)

Giggs made his debut with United as a seventeen-year-old,

and has proceeded to make the left midfield position his own, with his pace and dribbling causing near-constant torment for opposition defenses. His time with United has seen him win numerous trophies including nine league titles, four FA Cups, and a UEFA Champions League crown in 1999.

Yet while Giggs was winning everything with United, success with Wales proved elusive. The 1994 qualifying campaign came down to a final-day match at home with Romania that Wales had to win. With the score tied 1-1, Wales earned a penalty kick that was subsequently missed by Paul Bodin, and Romania went on to win 2-1. That was as close as Giggs would get to World Cup glory.

Manchester United's Ryan Giggs looks to penetrate the Aston Villa defense during a 2008 F.A. Cup match. While Giggs won numerous trophies during his career with the Red Devils, he was never able to lead the Welsh national team to a World Cup. *Jed Leicester/BPI and isiphotos.com*

8. JOSE MANUEL MORENO (ARGENTINA)

The burly forward was part of the River Plate sides of the '30s and '40s that were dubbed "La Maquina" (The Machine) for their goalscoring exploits, as well as winning five league titles between 1936 and 1945. Moreno went on to play in Colombia, Mexico, and Chile, winning titles in each league, becoming the first and only player to win championships in four different countries.

Moreno excelled at international level as well, leading Argentina to three Copa America titles in 1941, 1942, and 1947. But war and organizational politics conspired to keep him away from soccer's biggest tournament. Incensed over the fact that the 1938 World Cup would be held in Europe for the second time in a row, Argentina refused to enter. World War II and its aftermath prevented the tournament from being held in the '40s, and when Argentina also withdrew from the 1950 event, Moreno's World Cup shutout was complete.

9. IAN RUSH (WALES)

Like his countryman Giggs, Rush was unable to translate his brilliant club career into success at the international level. Rush was at the heart of the Liverpool sides that dominated English soccer in the '80s, winning five league titles, four FA Cups, and one European Cup. And with 326 goals, Rush remains Liverpool's all-time top goal-scorer.

Rush holds the same title for Wales, having tallied twenty-eight goals in seventy-eight appearances, but it wasn't enough to qualify them for a World Cup, as Wales thrice came within a razor's edge of qualifying. In addition to the aforementioned 1994 campaign, qualification in 1982 saw Wales lose out on goal difference to Czechoslovakia. The same fate awaited the Welsh in 1986, when a 1-1 draw with Scotland in their final match saw the Scots advance at Wales' expense.

10. DUNCAN EDWARDS (ENGLAND)

Edwards is a classic case of a player being cut down in his prime. At age twenty-one, Edwards had already been a professional for five years, leading the Manchester United sides of the early '50s, and had made eighteen international appearances for England. Yet before Edwards could light up a World Cup, he perished in a 1953 plane crash carrying the United side back from a European Cup match.

Such was Edwards' ability that England all-time leading scorer Bobby Charlton said that if he had to play one game for his life, and could pick one teammate, it would have been Edwards.

Best Teams That Didn't Win a World Cup

While the spoils are the exclusive property of the victors, the losers are usually left with nothing more than anonymity. And while winning the world's best-known trophy grants a team and their players sporting immortality, there have been plenty of other noteworthy teams who fell just short of soccer's ultimate prize.

1. HUNGARY (1954)

The Magical Magyars were blessed with some of the most breathtaking talent the world had ever seen. Ferenc Puskás, Sándor Kocsis, and Zoltán Czibor are still remembered as being the best of their era. Entering the 1954 World Cup, the Hungarians were heavy favorites, and when they dispatched Uruguay (who up to that point had never lost a World Cup match) 4-2 in the semifinals, the trophy appeared to be in their grasp. That's because their opponents in the final were West Germany, whom the Magyars had slaughtered 8-3 in the group phase. When Hungary went up 2-0 within the first ten minutes of the final, everything appeared to be going as planned. But ten minutes later the match was tied, and when Helmut Rahn scored with just six minutes to go, a colossal upset was in the making.

The final frantic minutes were littered with controversy. An apparent equalizer by Puskás was ruled out for offside, and a foul in the box on Kocsis went unpunished. When the final whistle blew, "The Miracle of Bern" was complete. Within two years, the Red Army would roll through Budapest, and soon after, Puskás, Kocsis, and Czibor would defect to Spain. Hungary would never again come so close to winning the World Cup.

2. **BRAZIL (1950)**

If a picture in the dictionary were needed for the word "hubris," a photo of the 1950 Brazil team would suffice. That year's World Cup tournament, hosted by Brazil, and the first one held following the end of World War II, was supposed to be the host nation's coming out party. And for the most part, it was. Brazil claimed top spot in their group, and the other three group winners advanced to the second phase of the tournament. But rather than use a knockout system, the second round used a round-robin format, with the winner being the team with the best record after three games. As luck would have it, the final group game was a de facto final, with Brazil and Uruguay squaring off. Brazil had won their two previous games by a combined score of 10-2 while Uruguay had snuck by with a tie against Spain and a narrow win against Sweden. All Brazil had to do was tie the match and the World Cup would be theirs.

So confident of victory were the Brazilians that prior to the match medals were made for each player, with their name engraved. A song commemorating the event was composed. Even Jules Rimet, the president of FIFA, got into the act, preparing a speech in Portuguese. And when Friaça put the hosts ahead just minutes into the second half, Brazil were in control. Even when Juan Schiaffino equalized for Uruguay, there were no worries. But Uruguay's Alcides Ghiggia broke through for the winner eleven minutes from time, and as the final whistle blew an eerie silence descended over the Maracanã Stadium. With little fanfare, Rimet was left to hand the trophy to Uruguayan captain Abdulio Valera.

3. THE NETHERLANDS (1974)

With the legendary Johann Cruyff at the controls, Holland dazzled the soccer world with a playing style dubbed "Total Football" in which players switched defending and attacking roles on the fly. During the first group stage, Holland staked their claim to the title with two victories and a draw. The second group stage saw the Dutch really hit their stride, as they dispatched reigning champions Brazil 2-0.

In the final, Holland was set to play the hosts West Germany, and the match could not have started any better. Straight from the kickoff, Holland kept possession, until Dieter Hoeness fouled Cruyff in the box after just two minutes. Johan Neeskens slammed home the ensuing penalty, and Holland was ahead 1-0. The goal was dubbed "The Poisoned Gift" as Holland, instead of adding to their advantage, opted to toy with the Germans. The approach proved fatal, as a penalty kick from Paul Breitner and a goal from Gerd Muller saw West Germany prevail with a 2-1 win and claim their second World Cup crown.

4. BRAZIL (1982)

This edition of the "Canarinho" had some of the finest attacking players of their day. Falcão, Socrates, and the incomparable Zico dazzled fans in the group stage with free-flowing, attack-minded soccer. In this tournament, the second stage was comprised of four groups of three, and when both Italy and Brazil defeated Argentina, their match was essentially a quarterfinal. It would turn out to be a classic. Because of their superior goal difference, Brazil only needed to tie the Italians, and despite trailing for most of the match, Falcão's equalizer in the sixty-eighth minute appeared to give the Brazilians the result they needed. But the favorites could not curb their attacking instincts, and were duly punished with sixteen minutes to play when Paolo Rossi rifled home his third goal of the game. Italy would go on to win their third World Cup, while in Brazil the match became known as "Sarria's Disaster," after the Barcelona stadium where the match took place.

5. ENGLAND (1970)

The then-reigning World Cup champions entered the 1970 tournament as joint favorites with Brazil, and with the likes of Bobby Moore, Gordon Banks, and Bobby Charlton reprising their roles from four years earlier, a repeat performance was expected. A 1-0 defeat at the hands of Brazil in group play was viewed as a minor hiccup, and England qualified for the knockout phase courtesy of wins over Czechoslovakia and Romania.

In a rematch of the 1966 final, England were paired with West Germany, and appeared to be cruising to victory when they took a 2-0 just four minutes into the second half. But manager Alf Ramsey made the fateful decision to remove Charlton "to spare him for the rest of the tournament." Without Charlton controlling the tempo, the Germans crawled back into the match, leveling through Franz Beckenbauer and Uwe Seeler, and then won the match in extra time on a goal by Gerd Muller.

6. PORTUGAL (1966)

The team was nicknamed "Os Magricos" after a fourteenth-century Portuguese knight who traveled to England with eleven colleagues to defend the virtue of twelve English women. Leading the charge six centuries later was Eusebio, who led the tournament with nine goals. But Portugal was far from a one-man team. Mário Coluna pulled the strings from midfield, while winger Antonio Simões added to the attack as well.

Portugal won all of their group games, including a 3-1 triumph over Brazil that eliminated the two-time defending champs from the tournament. The quarterfinal match against North Korea was the stuff of legend. The Asian up-starts raced to a 3-0 lead after just twenty-five minutes, but four goals by Eusebio in a thirty-two-minute span propelled Portugal to a 5-3 victory. Their march to the title was ended by hosts England 2-1, with Eusebio netting a late penalty.

7. ITALY (1994)

Entering the 1994 World Cup, Italy was on everyone's list of favorites. World Player of the Year Roberto Baggio was at his peak, while the likes of Franco Baresi and Paolo Maldini anchored the defense. What ensued was a roller coaster ride of stomach turning proportions. Italy began the tournament by losing to Ireland 1-0, and overcoming the ejection of goalkeeper Gianluca Pagliuca to defeat Norway 1-0, before gaining a 1-1 draw with Mexico. The results were only good enough for third place in the group, but the format that year allowed for the four best third-place teams to qualify for the knockout, and Italy squeaked through.

In the round of 16, they appeared on their way out to Nigeria, but Baggio, who had been anonymous up to that point, popped up for a late equalizer, and when Italy prevailed in overtime, they suddenly found their form, defeating Spain 2-1 and Bulgaria 2-0. The final against Brazil was expected to be a dazzling affair, but caution and dominant defense ruled the day. In the subsequent penalty shootout, Italian lynchpins Baresi and Baggio both missed their attempts, and Italy was denied their fourth World Cup title by the thinnest of margins.

8. FRANCE (1982)

With the legendary Michel Platini manning the controls, France entered the 1982 World Cup as a team on the rise. That is until England dispatched them 3-1 in the first match of the group phase. But the French regained their self-belief, finished second in the group, and with the exception of Brazil played some of the best soccer of the tournament.

In their way stood West Germany, and the match would end up as one of the most epic confrontations in the tournament's history. Regulation time ended 1-1, but was more notable for German goalkeeper Harald Schumacher's horrendous foul on Patrick Battiston that knocked the Frenchman out of the game, but went unpunished. In extra time, goals from Marius Trésor and Alain Giresse appeared to put France in the driver's seat, but tallies from Karl-Heinz Rummenigge and a spectacular bicycle kick from Klaus Fischer saw the Germans tie the score 3-3. Penalties beckoned, and West Germany would emerge triumphant, while the anguished French went home.

9. THE NETHERLANDS (1978)

This edition of "Clockwork Orange" played without the renowned Cruyff, who depending on whom you believe either boycotted the tournament because of actions by Argentina's ruling military junta, or simply retired because he thought he was past his prime. While the Dutch appeared to miss the talented midfielder in the first round, they hit top form in the second group phase with 1974 holdovers Rob Rensenbrink, Ruud Krol, and Johnny Rep all picking up the slack.

Argentine midfielder Juan Roman Riquelme (10) looks to evade a challenge from Germany's Torsten Frings during the quarterfinals of the 2006 FIFA World Cup. Argentina played some of the best soccer in the tournament, but their penalty kick shootout loss to Germany saw them go down as one of the best teams to fall short of winning a world championship.
Brad Smith/isiphotos.com

As in '74, Holland was fated to play the hosts in the final and fell short by an even slimmer margin than they did four years earlier. Mario Kempes had put the hosts up in the first half, but Dick Nanninga tied the match in the eighty-second minute. With Holland having all of the momentum, they went for the win, only to see Rensenbrink hit the post with just minutes to play. Argentina eventually prevailed in extra time on goals by Kempes and Daniel Bertoni, and Holland would never again come so close to claiming the trophy.

10. ARGENTINA (2006)

With midfield maestro Juan Román Riquelme at the controls, the Argentines waltzed through the opening round, displaying the kind of vibrant soccer that fans crave. Of note was a twenty-six-pass move that resulted in Esteban Cambiasso scoring the second goal in a 6-0 demolition of Serbia and Montenegro, as well as Maxi Rodriguez's thumping volley that secured a 2-1 overtime triumph in the round-of-sixteen against Mexico.

In the quarterfinals, Argentina faced hosts Germany, and when Roberto Ayala scored shortly after halftime, it appeared as though the South Americans might pull through. An untimely injury to goalkeeper Roberto Abbondanzieri forced Leonardo Franco to deputize, and ten minutes later German forward Miroslav Klose equalized. Argentine head coach Jose Pekerman then created a feast for second-guessers, taking off both Riquelme and forward Hernán Crespo near the end of regulation time. The game ended with Germany prevailing in a penalty kick shootout, and the team that had played perhaps the best soccer of the tournament was sent packing.

Most Capped Men

Longevity is a hallmark of most successful soccer careers, but staying in the game at the international level represents an even greater accomplishment. National team coaches come and go, and with them, their at-times fickle decisions regarding player selection. The opportunity to excel in international tournaments doesn't always present itself either, with injury or a loss of form often blunting a player's national team progress. That makes the accomplishments of these players, who made more international appearances than anyone, even more impressive.

1. MOHAMED AL-DEAYEA
There was a time when Al-Deayea dreamed of playing team handball rather than soccer, but Al-Deayea's brother Abdullah, a goalkeeper in his own right, convinced him to follow in his footsteps. What ensued is the longest career in the history of international soccer. The all-time leader with 181 international appearances, Al-Deayea made his debut with Saudi Arabia at the 1990 Asian Cup. His heroics in the 1996 version of the tournament, in which he led his country to penalty shootout wins in both the semifinal and final, represented his international peak.

Al-Deayea also participated in four World Cups, but along with Mexico's Antonio Carbajal, he holds the dubious distinction of conceding the most goals in the history of the finals, with twenty-five goals finding the back of his net. But Al-Deayea enjoyed some success at the World Cup as well, helping his side to the second round in 1994.

2. CLAUDIO SUAREZ

There was a time when "El Emperador" held the record for most international appearances, but he was caught and passed by Al-Deayea at the 2002 World Cup. Still, Suarez's mark of 178 caps remains the highest for an outfield player. He was a mainstay in the center of Mexico's defense for well over a decade, leading El Tri to three CONCACAF Gold Cup triumphs as well as appearances at the 1994, 1998, and 2006 World Cups.

3. HOSSAM HASSAN

Reading *War and Peace* might take less time than wading through the list of honors the Egyptian has won during a career that has lasted over twenty years. Hassan has claimed an incredible forty-one trophies during his career, and while most of those came at club level, Hassan has his share of international accolades as well, including three African Nations Cup triumphs.

But what the fiery striker will be best remembered for are his 170 appearances for Egypt, and his sixty-nine goals represent the sixth highest mark at international level. Even more remarkable is that Hassan's frequent feuds with some national team coaches, most notably Dutchman Ruud Krol, occasionally found him omitted from the national team. Otherwise Hassan might have found himself at the top of the list.

4. ADNAN AL-TALYANI

The forward from the United Arab Emirates is this list's Invisible Man. He spent his entire career playing in the UAE for one club, Al Shaab, and made his international debut in 1984, scoring in a 2-0 defeat of Kuwait in the Gulf Cup. For the next thirteen years, Al-Talyani was an ever-present force for the UAE, making 164 appearances, including three at the 1990 World Cup finals in Italy. When he retired in 1997, he did so as the all-time leader in international appearances.

5. COBI JONES

The dreadlocked attacker was never the best player on the American squad, but his 164 caps are testament to the consistency that Jones displayed during his career. The California native was forced to walk on to the soccer team at college powerhouse UCLA, but he rose through the ranks there, and his speed and dynamic runs on the wing eventually earned himself a berth in Bora Milutinovic's squad at the 1994 World Cup. Jones also appeared in the 1998 and 2002 World Cup finals and helped the United States win the CONCACAF Gold Cup in 2002.

6. SAMI AL-JABER

The Saudi playmaker checks in with 163 appearances, and his forty-four international goals are good enough to rank him in the Top 50 all-time. But Al-Jaber achieved some other notable honors as well. He is one of six players—and the first from Asia—to have scored a goal in three different World Cup finals, having done so in the 1994, 1998, and 2006 tournaments.

Al-Jaber's skill was evident even as a teenager, signing for Al-Hilal when he was fifteen years old. Just four years later, he made his first appearance for Saudi Arabia in a 1-1 draw against Syria in the Arab Cup.

7. MARTIN REIM
Almost from the moment Estonia regained its independence in 1991, Reim has been a fixture in midfield for the national side, earning 154 appearances (and counting). Put another way, Reim has only missed forty matches since Estonia resumed international play. But Reim is also owner of a more melancholy mark: He is the most capped player never to have played in the finals of a World Cup.

8. IVAN HURTADO
An elegant and incisive defender, Hurtado made his debut as a seventeen-year-old in 1985, becoming the youngest player to ever suit up for Ecuador. Since then, Hurtado has been a mainstay on Ecuador's backline with 155 caps. He starred in his country's unexpected run to the second round of the 2006 World Cup, and he holds the distinction of playing in more South American World Cup qualifying matches than any other player.

9. LOTHAR MATTHÄUS
Matthäus's ability on the field was matched only by his considerable ego, but there is no denying he is one of the game's greats. His 150 appearances for both West Germany and the unified German team included a World Cup triumph in 1990, which led to his being named FIFA Player of the Year. Matthäus also holds several individual international records. He is the only outfield player to have played in five World Cups, and he also holds the top spot with twenty-five games played at the finals.

10. **ALI DAEI**

The Iranian forward is the undisputed goal king of international men's soccer, scoring an incredible 109 goals in 149 appearances. Critics will contend that most of his strikes came against lesser competition, but Daei fashioned a respectable five-year career in Germany's Bundesliga, which speaks to the quality of the playmaker's game. Daei also participated in two World Cups with Iran, and played a pivotal part in his country's 2-1 triumph over the United States in 1998.

Most Capped Women

The first men's World Cup took place in 1930. The first women's edition took place over sixty years later. So who rules the roost in terms of total number of international appearances? The women, by far. In fact, the most-capped man would barely crack the top ten.

1. KRISTINE LILLY

The United Kingdom may have had Maggie Thatcher, but when it comes to international appearances, Lilly is soccer's "Iron Lady." Lilly hasn't been there for every game the U.S. women have played, but she's close. As of the end of 2007, Lilly had played in 340 of the Americans' 398 official internationals, passing the UAE's Adnan Al-Talyani in 1999 for the most caps. Lilly has also been on the field in every single World Cup and Olympic match the United States has played. And her 129 international goals are second most for either a man or a woman.

Despite her longevity, Lilly has often been in the background, and this was perfectly illustrated in the 1999 World Cup final against China. It was Lilly who headed a Chinese shot off the line in overtime, and she slotted home the third penalty kick in the epic shootout that followed, only for Brandi Chastain to get the glory.

2. MIA HAMM

While Hamm's 275 appearances are a bit short of Lilly's tally, her career mark of 158 international goals remains

U.S. forward Kristine Lilly celebrates her sixtieth-minute goal in the United States's 3-0 win over England in the quarterfinals of the 2007 FIFA Women's World Cup. Lilly has 340 national team appearances to her name, more than any other man or woman in international soccer. *Trent Davol/isiphotos.com*

the all-time record for any gender and contributed to her iconic status. Hamm made her first appearance as a fifteen-year-old in 1987, and while her goal-scoring exploits are legendary, she was equally adept at setting them up. Her 144 career assists are a record as well.

3. JULIE FOUDY

It's not for nothing that the U.S. captain was known as "Loudy Foudy," but far from just being the mouth that roared, Foudy backed it up on the field as well. During her 272 international appearances, she was one of the midfield engines that made the U.S team go.

Foudy also was one of the pioneers in the first incarnation of the WUSA, and it was during that time that her San Diego Spirit team went up against the San Jose CyberRays, who just happened to be coached by her husband, Ian Sawyers.

4. JOY FAWCETT

In addition to suiting up for the U.S. team 239 times, Fawcett gave new meaning to the term "soccer mom," as she returned to the field just three weeks after giving birth to her third child, Madilyn, in 2001. On that occasion, Fawcett barely missed a beat, which pretty much describes her entire international career, one that saw her hailed as the best defender in the world during an international career that spanned seventeen years.

5. TIFFENY MILBRETT

"Millie" is a nickname more reminiscent of a chain-smoking aunt than one of the most feared strikers in the world, but Milbrett was an absolute terror during her time with the U.S. national team, reaching 204 appearances. Of her 100 goals, none was bigger than her game-winning strike in the 1996 Olympics final.

Milbrett scored five goals against Panama on November 12, 2001, which tied the U.S. single-game record. Milbrett also holds the record for most assists in a game, getting five helpers in a 1997 match against Australia.

6. BRANDI CHASTAIN

Everyone knows about Chastain's bra-revealing celebration in the 1999 Women's World Cup final against China. Less well known is that Chastain began her international career as a forward, once scoring five goals in a game against Mexico, which at the time gave her the single-game record, a mark later tied by Milbrett and Michele Akers.

Chastain was later cut from the team but came back in 1996 as a defender, and was a mainstay through the 2004 Olympics, earning 192 caps in the process.

7. FAN YUNJIE

Were it not for Lilly's aforementioned heroics, Fan might very well have been the hero of the 1999 final, as it was her header that Lilly cleared off the line. But Fan still enjoyed a highly successful career, suiting up for China 192 times, and her goal in the 1998 Asian Games final gave China a 2-1 victory over North Korea. Fan later plied her trade in the WUSA for the San Diego Spirit.

8. HEGE RIISE

The United States had few rivals in the '90s, but Norway certainly qualified, losing in the inaugural World Cup final in 1991 to the Americans, but getting their revenge four years later when they took home the title. And at the center of it all was

Riise, whose physical presence and vision in midfield was instrumental to the Norwegians' success. Her contribution was recognized when she was named MVP of the 1995 World Cup.

Riise's longevity was borne out by her 188 international appearances, and she was still playing high-level soccer in the WUSA well into her thirties.

9. CHRISTIE RAMPONE

While most players on the U.S. national team hailed from powerhouse collegiate programs, Rampone played at tiny Monmouth University, mostly because the school allowed her to play both basketball and soccer. But acting on a tip, head coach Tony DiCicco watched Rampone play and invited her to training camp, and with both Joy Fawcett and Carla Overbeck out on maternity leave, Rampone settled in at right back and has been impossible to dislodge since, tallying 183 caps by the middle of 2008.

10. ZHAO LIHONG

Another member of the famed Chinese teams of the '90s, "The Cat" was tabbed by many as the best left-sided women's player in the world, even though she often played in the shadow of star striker Sun Wen. But Zhao's crossing ability and skill off the dribble were vital to China's success, so much so that she played 182 times for her national side. And American fans got to see Zhao's skills up close in 2002 when she played for the WUSA's Philadelphia Charge.

The "Other" Competitions

The good folks at FIFA would have you believe that the soccer world begins and ends with tournaments sanctioned under their auspices, but the vast net cast by the game has spawned numerous lesser-known competitions. Some are humorous, others inspiring, but all of them add plenty of color to the world's most popular sport.

1. CLERICUS CUP

The tournament, a gathering of sixteen teams comprised solely of Catholic priests and seminarians, meets at the Vatican every year to crown a champion. Redemptis Mater College prevailed over Pontifical Lateran University in the tournament's inaugural edition in 2007, and lest anyone think that priests would take a more dispassionate view toward competition need only have watched the final. In that match, the Redemptis Mater striker won a late penalty amid claims that he had dived. When several Pontifical Lateran players remonstrated with the referee, they earned blue cards that resulted in a trip to the "original sin bin" in which players committing too many fouls are forced to leave the field for a few minutes. This prompted the Italian newspaper *La Stampa* to issue the headline, "Priestly footballers?

Worse than Materazzi," in reference to the rugged Italian defender victimized by Zinedine Zidane's head-butt in the 2006 World Cup final.

2. HOMELESS WORLD CUP
To bring attention to the plight of the world's homeless, Mel Young, editor of Scottish street paper *The Big Issue*, and Harald Schmied, editor of the Austrian-based publication *Megafon,* began the Homeless World Cup, which has been held every year since 2003. The rules stipulate that to be eligible a player must have been homeless at some point during the last year, be seeking political asylum, or make his income selling street papers. The number of participating teams has grown from eighteen to forty-eight since the tournament's inception, with Scotland triumphing in the 2007 event. The 2008 edition will be held in Australia.

3. TOLSTOY CUP
John Lennon once crooned, "Give peace a chance," but that advice doesn't get much traction in the annual battle between Bradford University's Peace Studies FC and Kings College London's War Studies FC. In the first edition in 2007, the two-legged affair ended 1-1, with Peace overcoming War 4-3 on penalties. Around £250 was raised for charity.

4. BLIND WORLD CUP
So how does a blind person play soccer? Simple. The ball has pieces of metal inside so players can hear the ball as it approaches them. Fans are encouraged to be quiet so the players can hear the ball as well as their coach's instructions on when to shoot. The goalkeepers are the only sighted players, while the field players are blindfolded so that those with partial vision will be without eyesight of any kind. But

while the rules and participants may be different, the usual suspects have come out on top in the Blind World Cup. In 2006, hosts Argentina defeated Brazil 1-0.

5. ROBOCUP

Think a team of robots could beat Italy or Brazil? It may sound like something out of *I, Robot,* but a group of robotics researchers are aiming to do just that by the middle of the twenty-first century. In the meantime, in an effort to promote research in robotics and artificial intelligence the robots of today play against each other in RoboCup, a soccer tournament with several divisions (simulation, small, medium, four-legged, and humanoid) that has been held every year since 1997. And while teams from China, Germany, Australia, and the United States took home various prizes in the 2007 edition, it was a team from Osaka, Japan, that won the Humanoid Division. Isaac Asimov, eat your heart out.

6. AMPUTEE WORLD CUP

Proof that there are no obstacles to playing soccer is evident in the Amputee World Cup, which was started in 2005 and is open to field players missing a leg as well as goalkeepers missing an arm. The field players move about with the help of crutches but are not allowed to use them to control or pass the ball. The last edition of the tournament was held in 2007, with Uzbekistan prevailing over Russia 2-1.

7. BEACH SOCCER WORLD CUP

Contrary to popular belief, FIFA's motto is not, "We are FIFA. You will be assimilated. Resistance is futile." Nonetheless, what started out as a Brazilian invention in 1995 was taken over by FIFA in 2005. But no matter who has run the tournament, Brazil has been the master of the five-on-five beach format, winning eleven of the thirteen tournaments held. Only Portugal in 2001, and France, with a certain Eric Cantona at the helm in 2005, has managed to escape Brazil with victories. The 2008 edition will be held outside of Brazil for the first time, with France assuming the role of hosts.

8. FIFI WILD CUP

While FIFA rules the roost in world football, not every part of the world can gain membership, with political concerns often preventing various countries from participating in a World Cup. But all is not lost because FIFI, the Federation of International Football Independents, has created its own World Cup for the likes of Tibet, Greenland, and Zanzibar. The last such competition was held in Hamburg, Germany, at the same time as the real World Cup, with the home stadium of club side St. Pauli as the venue. While the home-based Republic of St. Pauli made it all the way to the semifinals, it was the Turkish Republic of North Cyprus who prevailed on penalties over Zanzibar 4-1 after normal time ended scoreless.

9. MURATTI

In this competition between the English Channel Islands of Guernsey, Jersey, and Alderney, familiarity has bred more than just contempt in over 100 years of competition. Each year, the cup holder awaits the winner of the first round match between the other two contestants. The competition has even seen the likes of former England internationals Graeme Le Saux and Matthew Le Tissier squaring off for Jersey and Guernsey, respectively. Of the ninety-one times the tournament has been held (it was suspended during the two world wars), Jersey has prevailed forty-eight times, Guernsey on forty-two occasions, with Alderney claiming the trophy just once back in 1920.

10. **THE PELADÃO**

"Brazil has three loves, one is [soccer], the other is women, the third is beer," so said Dissica Calderaro in an interview with the publication, *Latin Trade*. Calderaro would know because it was his father, Umberto, who in 1972 found a way to combine all three elements in the Peladão, an amateur soccer tournament held every year in the Amazonian city of Manaus. The tournament has an important twist, however. Not only does each of the over 900 participating teams bring players and coaches, but they bring a beauty queen, complete with support staff as well. If the team is eliminated in the early rounds but the beauty queen advances, the team is allowed back into the tournament. Professional models are not allowed to take part, although one winner went on to become Miss Brazil. Calderaro added, "Peladão is a city party—everyone gets involved."

Ageless Wonders

"Never trust anyone over thirty" may have been one of the rallying cries of the '60s, but it's a philosophy that seems to have been hijacked by soccer clubs the world over, who seem eager to unload a player once they hit that threshold of decrepitude. Some players, however, have managed to thrive in their Golden Years, proving that they can still teach the youngsters a thing or two.

1. SIR STANLEY MATTHEWS
At the tender age of thirty-two, Matthews was asked by his manager, Blackpool's Joe Smith, if he could carry on playing for a few more years. Matthews managed that and more, playing in the English top flight until he was fifty. Matthews was also the oldest player to appear for England, which he did in 1957 at the age of forty-two. So what was the secret to Matthews' longevity? The simple answer was a training regimen that was way ahead of its time in terms of nutrition and discipline. He didn't drink or smoke, and he fasted for one day a week.

2. ROGER MILLA
At age thirty-five, Milla did what any normal soccer player

would do: he retired from international soccer. But in 1990, Cameroon's president, Paul Biya, convinced Milla that his country needed him one last time, and Milla agreed to come out of retirement and play at the 1990 World Cup. Milla went on to score four goals at that tournament, leading Cameroon to the quarterfinals and setting a mark for the oldest goalscorer in World Cup history. Milla wasn't done, however, as he returned in 1994, scoring Cameroon's lone goal in a 5-1 loss to Russia. On that day, Milla was forty-two years old, increasing his record as the oldest player ever to tally at a World Cup.

Cameroon's Roger Milla in action against Brazil during the 1994 FIFA World Cup. When Milla scored in a subsequent group match against Russia, he became the oldest goalscorer in World Cup history. *Tony Marshall/ EMPICS Sports Photo Agency*

3. **MACDONALD TAYLOR**

On March 31, 2004, an otherwise nondescript World Cup qualifier pitted the U.S. Virgin Islands against St. Kitts and Nevis. St. Kitts and Nevis thumped their Caribbean neighbors 7-0 on their way to an 11-0 aggregate victory. While the USVI had plenty of problems in defense, little blame was placed at the feet of defender MacDonald Taylor, who at the incredible age of forty-six took part in the day's proceedings, thus becoming the oldest player ever to appear in a World Cup qualifying match.

4. **BILLY MEREDITH**

While Taylor's exploits will be difficult to beat, for many years the title of oldest international player fell to Meredith, a Welshman whose career began in the late 1800s. Meredith was considered to be the first "soccer superstar," enjoying a stellar club career with both Manchester City and Manchester United. He was also one of the first performers to organize a players' union to combat the maximum wage of £4 a week. At international level, Meredith appeared forty-eight times for Wales, with the last of these occurring in a 1920 win against England at age forty-five. Meredith's club career lasted even longer, as he appeared in the FA Cup for Manchester City at age forty-nine.

5. **ROMARIO**

The Brazilian World Cup-winner celebrated his fortieth birthday in 2006, but that didn't stop him from banging in the goals for Rio-based club side Vasco de Gama. The source of Romario's motivation was to score one thousand goals in his career, a mark exceeded only by the legendary Pelé, and according to Romario, he finally reached the milestone in May 2007. Of course, Romario included in his tally those goals he scored at junior level as well as in friendlies. When he announced his retirement in April 2008 at the age of forty-two, his total in competitive fixtures left him around seventy goals short of his goal. Still, Romario remains one of the all-time great strikers.

6. PEDRO RIBEIRO LIMA

Ribeiro's strike rate isn't quite as prolific as Romario's was, but at least he can say he stuck around longer than the Brazilian legend. In April 2007 at the age of fifty-eight, Ribeiro scored for Brazilian club side Perilima. The goal came courtesy of a penalty kick during Perilima's 5-1 loss to Campinese during a Paraibano state championship match. Of course, it helped that Ribeiro is also the club's owner and founder.

7. JOHN RYAN

Ribeiro was by no means the first owner to put himself in the lineup. Ryan, the chairman of English minor league outfit Doncaster Rovers, pulled the same maneuver during the last game of the 2002–03 season, coming on for the last minute of the Rovers' 4-2 win over Hereford. The fact that Doncaster had already qualified for the playoffs made the substitution even less risky, as did the fact that he didn't even touch the ball. But at fifty-two years, eleven months, Ryan became the oldest player to feature in a competitive match in England.

8. KNUT OLAV FOSSLEIN

No such conflict of interest was evident with regard to Fosslein. In 2005, the Norwegian was plying his trade in the third division for FK Toten at the ripe old age of sixty.

Fosslein's debut came over forty years ago, and he's played in over 1,000 Norwegian league matches.

9. MARCO BALLOTTA

The Italian goalkeeper has made numerous pit stops during a career that has spanned twenty-five years, playing for nine different clubs. But his latest stint with Lazio saw him set two distinguished marks. In May 2006, Ballotta's appearance in the season finale against Ascoli saw him surpass Dino Zoff as the oldest player in Serie A history. Four months later, Ballotta did one better, when his appearance against Olympiakos saw him become the oldest player ever to participate in a UEFA Champions League match.

10. DINO ZOFF

When Zoff captained Italy to victory in the 1982 World Cup, it marked the third time that the side had won the title, matching their efforts in the 1934 and 1938 tournaments. But in the process, Zoff set a personal mark that still stands. At forty years of age, he is the oldest World Cup winner to date.

Precocious Talents

"It's a man's game," or so the saying goes. But that hasn't stopped a fair number of teenagers from strutting their stuff on the world stage and playing well beyond their years. Some of these performers went on to even bigger things while others struggled to build on their early success.

1. PELÉ
It was at the 1958 World Cup that the world was introduced to the then-seventeen-year-old Brazilian, who proceeded to set numerous records for a young player. Pelé's goal against Wales in a 1-0 quarterfinal victory still makes him youngest goalscorer at the tournament. His appearance in that year's final made him the youngest player in a World Cup title game, and his goal in the fifty-fifth minute made him the youngest goalscorer in a final as well.

2. NORMAN WHITESIDE
The man from Northern Ireland finally bettered one of Pelé's marks at the 1982 World Cup, when at seventeen years, forty-one days, Whiteside's appearance against Yugoslavia made him the youngest player to appear in the tournament's final stage. Whiteside later went on to play in the 1986 World

Cup as well, scoring in Northern Ireland's 1-1 tie with Austria. But despite his early success, a string of knee injuries saw him make just thirty-eight international appearances, and by age twenty-six Whiteside was forced to retire.

3. SOULEYMANE MAMAM
According to FIFA's official website, Mamam's international debut during Togo's World Cup qualifier against Zambia in May 2001 made him, at 13 years, 310 days, the youngest player to suit up in a qualifying match. But some sources, notably the website of Mamam's Belgian club, Royal Antwerp, list his birthday as 1985, not 1987, which would have made him almost sixteen at the time. Despite the discrepancy, Mamam remains the record holder in the eyes of all-knowing FIFA.

4. DIEGO MARADONA
Dieguito first lined up for Argentinos Juniors as a fifteen-year-old back in 1976 and led his team to the league title that season. Two years later, Maradona was the youngest top scorer in Argentina's top division. By that time, he had already made his international debut, making his first appearance on February 27, 1977, in a 5-1 demolition of Hungary. At that point, it looked like Maradona might eclipse some of Pelé's World Cup records at the 1978 edition of the tournament, but Maradona was the last player cut from the Argentine squad and had to watch as they won their first crown. Maradona didn't miss out entirely, however, as he went on to play in four World Cups and led the Albiceleste to victory in 1986.

5. DIEGO SUAREZ
Only a fourteen-year-old could play for a club called

Blooming, but the notoriety of Suarez extends even further. In January 2007, the midfielder became the youngest player to appear in a Copa Libertadores match when the Bolivian club fell 1-0 to Santos, a match where Suarez found himself marking their Brazilian World Cup midfielder, Ze Roberto. Like all young South American protégés, Suarez soon found himself on his way to Europe, where he is now on the books of Dynamo Kiev.

6. WAYNE ROONEY
Rooney has seemed destined to set numerous "youngest ever" records, only for them to be immediately surpassed. In 2002, his goal as a sixteen-year-old against Arsenal made him the youngest scorer in the EPL's history, only to see it beaten two months later by Leeds United's James Milner. Rooney went on to become the youngest goalscorer at a European Championship, scoring twice in 2004 against Switzerland, only for Swiss striker Johan Vonlanthen to beat his mark just four days later. But there is still one mark Rooney still holds, that being the youngest England goalscorer, which he accomplished in a Euro 2004 qualifier against Macedonia.

7. PAULINO ALCANTARA
Barcelona's all-time leading scorer wasn't born in Spain, but in the Philippines, and made his league debut back in 1912 at just fifteen years of age, scoring a hat trick against Catalá SC in a Catalonian League match. Alcantara went on to score an incredible 357 goals in as many matches, and he still holds the Barcelona marks for youngest player and youngest goalscorer.

8. SERGIO AGUERO
The Argentine currently plies his trade for Atletico Madrid,

but back in 2003 he made his club debut for Independiente, and at fifteen years, thirty-five days, he set a record for the youngest player to perform in Argentina's top flight, exceeding Maradona's mark. In 2006, Aguero made his debut for Argentina at senior level and led their U-20 side to victory at the 2007 U-20 World Cup, winning the Golden Ball as the tournament's best player.

9. PETER OFORIQUAYE

The Ghanaian joined the professional ranks at the tender age of fifteen, signing for Greek side Kalamata FC. Just two years later, he joined the giants of Greek soccer, Olympiakos, and proceeded to make history during the 1997–98 season. On October 1, 1997, Olympiakos were in the process of getting thrashed 5-1 by Norwegian side Rosenborg in that year's UEFA Champions League. But their only goal was scored by Oforiquaye, who at seventeen years, 195 days, became the youngest goalscorer in Champions League history.

10. FREDDY ADU

There had been American soccer phenoms before, but none of them shouldered the weight of expectations like Adu did on April 3, 2004, when the fourteen-year-old made his professional debut for D.C. United against the San Jose Earthquakes. The appearance made Adu the youngest American in over a century to appear in any team sport. Success has been hard to come by since then, although Adu, at age sixteen, did become the youngest player to suit up for the U.S. national team when he appeared in a January 2006 friendly against Canada. Adu has since moved on to Portuguese side Benfica, where at the age of eighteen, he became the youngest American to appear in the UEFA Champions League.

Great Keepers

In his autobiography, *Cloughie: Walking on Water*, legendary manager Brian Clough said of goalkeepers, "I've never fathomed why top keepers don't cost as much as top strikers. A save can be as important as a goal, but a mistake by a keeper is often more costly than a miss at the other end."

If wages are anything to go by, keepers are still an underappreciated group, but there have been a fair few who have made their case as the most important player on the field.

1. LEV YASHIN

The man they called "The Black Spider" for his all-black outfits, Yashin helped revolutionize the position, in that he was one of the first to command the entire eighteen-yard-box. The Moscow native was also renowned for his reflexes and is rumored to have saved more than 150 penalty kicks in his twenty-two-year career. Such ability saw Yashin named the European Player of the Year in 1963, the only goalkeeper to have won the award. Yashin was also named to numerous all-century teams, and the trophy for the World Cup's outstanding goalkeeper bears his name.

2. GORDON BANKS

The save Banks pulled off against Pelé in the 1970 World Cup is widely regarded as the greatest of all-time, when he managed to deflect the Brazilian's downward header up and over the bar. Banks later admitted that it wasn't until applause began to ring out around the stadium in Guadalajara that he realized he had actually prevented a goal. Banks pulled off plenty of other fine saves during his career and backstopped England to the 1966 World Cup title.

Banks's status as England's top keeper ended in October 1972 when he lost his right eye in a car accident. Miraculously, Banks soldiered on, playing for the Ft. Lauderdale Strikers of the North American Soccer League, where he earned all-league honors in 1978.

3. DINO ZOFF

For all of the talk of goalkeepers being eccentrics, Zoff's calm and stoicism were the rock of some of Italy's most storied teams. He appeared in an Italian record 332 consecutive games for Juventus in the '70s and '80s, at one point going 903 minutes without conceding a goal. He was to eclipse that mark at international level, racking up 1,143 consecutive shutout minutes between 1972 and 1974. But Zoff's finest hour came when he captained Italy to the 1982 World Cup, becoming just the second goalkeeper, along with compatriot Gianpiero Combi, to captain his side to victory.

4. SEPP MAIER

Maier was as peculiar as Zoff was reserved. Not only did his outsized gloves and shorts convey the clown in him, but it wasn't unusual for Maier to engage in some Harlem Globetrotter-like ball tricks when claiming the ball in his area. Yet "The Cat" was also ruthlessly effective in goal. Maier appeared in 422 consecutive matches for Bayern Munich, and that streak remains a German league record. He also helped Bayern to three European Cup triumphs as well as numerous league and cup crowns along the way. Maier reached his peak in the 1974 World Cup final, when he helped West Germany defeat Holland 2-1 in his home stadium in Munich.

5. PETER SCHMEICHEL

It seemed as if Schmeichel's career credo was "I'm mad as hell, and I'm not going to take it anymore," such was the ferocity with which he bellowed at his defense. But the Dane had the ability to back up his verbal tirades and was twice named the World's Best Goalkeeper by the International Federation of Football History and Statistics (IFFHS) in 1992 and 1993. His six-foot-four inch frame made him an intimidating presence in goal, and his massive throws sparked many a counterattack for Manchester United, with whom he spent his most productive years, including the treble-winning season of 1998–99. Schmeichel also led Denmark to the 1992 European Championships.

6. JOSE LUIS CHILAVERT

While most keepers are known for stopping goals, Chilavert, with his thunderous free kicks and penalties, was equally well-known for scoring them. He was also known as a hot-head, earning a three-game international suspension in 1998 for spitting at Brazilian defender Roberto Carlos. All of this served to overshadow the fact that Chilavert was outstanding in goal. Like Schmeichel, his height of six-foot-four was enough to discourage even the bravest of forwards from entering his goal area, and his reflexes were top notch.

He was thrice named World Goalkeeper of the Year by the IFFHS and took top goalkeeping honors at the 1998 World Cup.

7. PAT JENNINGS
Born in County Down, Northern Ireland, Jennings honed his goalkeeping skills playing another sport, Gaelic football. Having hands the size of shovels helped, but Jennings also showed an uncanny ability to save shots with his feet, a skill rare in the English leagues of the '60s and '70s where he enjoyed immense success at Tottenham Hotspur as well as arch-rivals Arsenal. Jennings also was indispensable for the Northern Ireland national team, leading the tiny country to the second round of the 1982 World Cup as well as the 1986 tournament in Mexico.

8. AMADEO CARRIZO
Before goalkeepers like Jorge Campos and Rene Higuita wowed fans with their forays out of the goal, there was Carrizo. The Argentine was a fixture for Buenos Aires club River Plate from 1945 to 1968 and played professionally well into his forties. And his willingness to dribble out of his box and start the attack had heretofore been unheard of. Internationally, the player known as "Tarzan" had less success, as his career coincided with a relative down period in Argentine soccer, but his exploits at club level saw him widely recognized as one of the all-time greats.

9. UBALDO FILLOL
You wouldn't expect a player nicknamed "The Duck" to be among the legends in the game, but Fillol's career of twenty-plus years certainly qualifies him as such, especially in Argentine soccer circles. Fillol forged his reputation with

the River Plate teams of the '70s, but he is best known for his performances with the Argentine national team that took home the 1978 World Cup trophy on home soil. He made a key penalty save in the second round against Poland, and in the final against the Netherlands he did much to keep the visitors at bay. Fillol's international career ended in 1985, but he continued to play into his forties, finishing his career with Argentinean side Velez Sarsfield.

10. PETER SHILTON

Shilton is best remembered for being on the receiving end of Diego Maradona's "Hand of God" goal at the 1986 World Cup, but the Englishman also enjoyed many happier moments in a career that spanned an incredible thirty years. Shilton played in over 1,000 professional matches, and his 125 international appearances are an English record. The peak of Shilton's career occurred with Nottingham Forest in the late '70s and early '80s, when he helped them to two European Cup titles. Shilton also shares the mark with France's Fabien Barthez for the most shutouts at the World Cup, with ten clean sheets to his name. As for the most international shutouts ever, Shilton has that mark all to himself, with sixty-six.

Dynasties

As much as the game's best players are celebrated, the same is true for teams from a certain era, especially those who were successful both on the domestic and international fronts.

1. REAL MADRID, 1953–1966
Trying to pick a golden era for Real is like trying to select the prettiest rose, such has been their success over the years. But in this thirteen-year span, Real Madrid dominated Spanish and European soccer like no other team has before or since. With the help of players like Alfredo di Stefano, Madrid won Spain's La Liga nine times, while hoisting the European Cup on six occasions, including the first five times the trophy was contested.

2. LIVERPOOL, 1975–1990
The Reds are the most successful English side to date, but the period encompassing the '70s and '80s qualifies as their Golden Age. In that time, Liverpool won the English championship ten times, while adding two FA Cups, one UEFA Cup, and four European Cups to their trophy cabinet. It was legendary coach Bill Shankly who laid the foundations

for these teams, with managers Bob Paisley, Joe Fagan, and Kenny Dalglish carrying on Shankly's tradition. Dalglish also played for many of the sides during this era, with performers like Alan Hansen and Ian Rush also playing crucial roles during that time.

3. SANTOS, 1960s

This was the time of Pelé, and while "The King" was instrumental in the team's success during this time, players like Coutinho and Pepe did their bit as well, with Coutinho scoring over 350 goals for the club. When they weren't traveling the world playing exhibitions, Santos were dominating Brazilian football, winning eight Paulista state titles, as well as two Copa Libertadores and two Intercontinental Cups. Santos also triumphed five times in the Taça Brazil, a knockout competition that at the time determined the Brazilian national champion.

4. AJAX, 1965–1973

Just as Pelé took Santos to its greatest heights, Johan Cruyff did the same for Dutch side Ajax. Cruyff led the Amsterdam-based club to six league titles in an eight-year span, but it was the three consecutive European Cup titles that cemented the team's place in the history books. Ajax had lost the European Cup Final in 1969, but the team finally broke through in 1971 when they defeated Greek side Panathinaikos 2-0.

By this time, head coach Rinus Michaels had instituted his Total Football scheme, but even after he left in 1971 to take up the reigns at Barcelona, Ajax's success continued, winning two more European crowns with a group of players known as "The Twelve Apostles." When Cruyff followed his mentor to Barca in 1973, Ajax's reign of dominance came to an end.

5. MANCHESTER UNITED, 1992–2003

While the '70s and '80s belonged to Liverpool, the '90s and early part of the new millennium belonged to United, who won the Premier League eight times in an eleven-year span. United also won "The Treble" in 1999 when they won the League, FA Cup, and UEFA Champions League in the same season. While David Beckham came to prominence during this period, it was players like Roy Keane, Eric Cantona, and Paul Scholes who were the lynchpins of the side.

6. PENAROL, 1960s

Los Manyas were the dominant Uruguayan side of the '60s, winning seven national titles. But Penarol also excelled at the international level, winning three Copa Libertadores crowns, including the first two times the trophy was contested. They also claimed the Intercontinental Cup when they defeated Benfica in 1961 and Real Madrid five years later. In an era when playing outside one's home country was rare, Penarol benefited from having two dominant foreigners on their roster, Ecuadorian forward Alberto Spencer and Peruvian winger Juan Joya.

7. JUVENTUS, 1971–1986

The "Old Lady" of Italian soccer has enjoyed several remarkable periods in her history, including a spell of five consecutive titles in the '30s. But their run of nine titles in fifteen seasons beginning in 1971 ranks among the most impressive periods of the modern era. Also remarkable is the way some of the team's greatest players book-ended this stretch. In 1971, performers such as striker Roberto Bettega and defender Franco Causio led the charge. By period's end, it was the talents of Michel Platini and Paolo Rossi that carried the day. The latter duo helped Juventus win their first European Cup in 1985, an event marred by the death of thirty-nine Juventus fans that perished when a retaining wall collapsed on top of them.

8. INDEPENDIENTE, 1970–1978

When one thinks of Argentine soccer, clubs like Boca Juniors and River Plate immediately come to mind, and while those two teams have won the most championships in Argentine soccer, the Independiente teams of the '70s bear special mention. Not only did the Red Devils win four Argentine championships during this period, but they are the only side to have won four consecutive Copa Libertadores, having done so from 1972 to 1975. At the heart of these teams was playmaker, Ricardo Bochini, who might have gone onto greater international renown had he not played the same position as a certain Diego Maradona.

9. CELTIC, 1966–1974

For sheer consistency, the Celtic teams of this time would have been difficult to match. Led by legendary manager Jock Stein, as well as players like Billy MacNeil and Jimmy "Jinky" Johnstone, the Bhoys won an incredible nine consecutive Scottish league titles, five Scottish Cups, and five League Cups. Their greatest moment came in 1967 when they won every competition they entered, including a 2-1 defeat of Inter Milan in that year's European Cup final. The match was held in Lisbon, Portugal, and the side was forever after known as "The Lisbon Lions."

10. RANGERS, 1989–1997

The aforementioned mark by Celtic set a world record for consecutive championships at the time, and it was one that would be equaled roughly twenty years later by their bitter

Glasgow rivals, the Rangers. The run began under manager Graeme Souness, but most of the success was achieved under Walter Smith. The Blues best season during that time came in 1993 when they won all three major Scottish competitions, but fell just short of matching Celtic's European Cup triumph when French side Marseille edged them out for a spot in the final.

Size Doesn't Matter

One of the best qualities of soccer is that attributes like height and strength aren't limiting factors. The two greatest players of all, Pelé and Diego Maradona, were both under five-foot-nine. The same goes for constructing national teams, where a large population doesn't guarantee international success. It doesn't matter if a country has a hundred great players; only that their best eleven get the job done, and often all it takes is one special generation of players to send a team to the greatest of international heights.

1. URUGUAY

The country that has struck perhaps the biggest blow for the little guy has been Uruguay, which despite having a population of fewer than 3.5 million, has twice claimed soccer's biggest prize. Le Celeste captured the inaugural World Cup title in 1930, and in 1950 they delivered one of the biggest World Cup shocks ever in defeating hosts Brazil 2-1 to claim their second championship.

The ensuing World Cups haven't been as kind to Uruguay, although they did qualify eight more times, and even made the semifinals in 1954 and in 1970. Still, Uruguay remains the smallest country ever to have hoisted the World Cup trophy.

2. TRINIDAD AND TOBAGO

After enduring qualifying heartbreak in 1974 and 1990, T&T finally broke through in 2006. The Soca Warriors went through a marathon campaign that ended with them going to a two-game playoff against Bahrain. A tie in the first leg at home didn't bode well, but Dennis Lawrence's goal in the return match allowed T&T to punch their ticket to the finals at last.

With a population of just over 1.3 million (that's about the same size as San Antonio, Texas), T&T became the smallest nation ever to qualify for the World Cup finals.

3. NORTHERN IRELAND

T&T's record was previously held by Northern Ireland, but the Irish still hold a number of distinctions. With a population topping 1.7 million, Northern Ireland remains the smallest country to have won their group in World Cup finals, having done so in 1982 at the expense of hosts Spain. "Norn Iron" is also the smallest country to have qualified for the finals more than once, having done so in 1958, 1982, and 1986.

4. COSTA RICA

Checking in at 4.3 million people, Costa Rica is another country that has belied its minnow status. This was especially true in 1990, when on their first trip to the finals the Ticos shocked heavily favored Scotland and Sweden to qualify for the second round, where they eventually fell to Czechoslovakia 4-1. Costa Rica followed up their efforts in 1990 by also qualifying in 2002 and 2006.

5. CROATIA

After Croatia gained its independence from Yugoslavia in 1992, one wouldn't have expected a nation of around 4.5

million people to make that much of an impression on the world soccer stage. But Croatia has long produced quality players, and its first attempt at World Cup glory in 1998 proved to be a memorable one. A generation led by striker Davor Suker and midfielder Zvonimir Boban took Croatia to the semifinals where they ultimately fell to hosts France 2-1. Even with the subsequent retirements of Suker and Boban, Croatia has remained a force in world soccer, having qualified for the 2002 and 2006 editions of the tournament as well.

6. SLOVENIA
For head coach Srecko Katanec about the only thing tougher than qualifying for the World Cup was managing temperamental striker Zlatko Zahovic, who when he wasn't tormenting opposition defenses, was trying his coach's patience. Following Slovenia's first match against Spain in the 2002 World Cup finals, Katanec sent Zahovic home for insubordination, causing despair in the home country and euphoria in the broadcast booth. Katanec resigned immediately after the tournament, and while Zahovic returned, Slovenia's two million inhabitants haven't had a reason to celebrate since.

7. SCOTLAND
The good: the Scots have qualified eight times for soccer's biggest party, giving the 5.1 million strong Tartan Army something to celebrate. The bad: They've never made it out of the first round, thrice going out on goal difference, and it was the 1978 squad featuring such stalwarts as Kenny Dalglish and Archie Gemmill that did the most to disappoint.

8. HUNGARY
When Italy won its second World Cup title in 1938, it was

Hungary who was on the losing end. When the aforementioned Magical Magyars of 1954 fell to Germany in the title decider as well, Hungary earned the dubious distinction of being the first country to lose two finals. The subsequent defections of players following the Soviet invasion of 1956 meant that the cream of Hungary's Golden Generation never suited up for them again. But for a country of 10.1 million, their exploits remain impressive.

q. CZECHOSLOVAKIA

The country may not exist anymore, but that didn't stop it from reaching (and losing) two World Cup finals in 1934 and 1962. The Czechoslovakians even led in both matches, but Italy rallied to win 2-1 in extra time in 1934, while Brazil overcame Josep Masopust's early goal to win the 1962 final 3-1.

Even with the subsequent split of the country, the Czech Republic has maintained the region's soccer tradition, qualifying for the World Cup in 2006 and making the final of the 1996 European Championships.

10. THE NETHERLANDS

The Netherlands is far from the smallest nation in FIFA, but at 16.1 million souls the Dutch aren't exactly massive either, and the number of internationally renowned players the country produces defies belief. Its performance in World Cups has belied its small size as well, having reached consecutive finals in 1974 and 1978. And in Johan Cruyff, the country produced one of the greatest players the sport has ever seen.

The Innovators

There have been numerous coaches who have enjoyed success, but only a select few can rightly claim to have changed the course of the world's most popular sport. Some achieved their aims through radical new approaches to tactics, while preparation and attention to detail gave other sides an edge. Either way, here are the trendsetters who brought the game forward.

1. HERBERT CHAPMAN

Given the ultra-defensive nature the game can sometimes take these days, it's shocking to think that back in the '20s teams played with just two dedicated defenders. This was due in part to the fact that the offside rule at the time required three players—not the present day two—to keep an opponent onside. But when the rule changed in 1925, a goal bonanza ensued, and it was left to Arsenal's Chapman, along with defender Charlie Buchan, to solve the problem. This was done by dropping an extra man into defense, and thus the "WM" formation of three defenders, two midfielders, and five (yes, five) forwards was born. Success wasn't instantaneous, but Arsenal went on to dominate the '30s, winning five league titles and two FA Cups. Soon thereafter, the formation was copied by the entire soccer world.

2. KARL RAPPAN

In Italian, it's called *catenaccio*, or "the bolt," and it involves using a defender, or "sweeper," to play behind three or even four man-marking defenders. The sweeper's role was to simply defend any attack that broke through the line in front of him. And while it achieved its greatest fame in Italy, the system was first conceived by an Austrian manager plying his trade in Switzerland during the '30s. Rappan first thought of the idea as a means of using an organized defense to combat teams with superior ability, and he used it with success at Swiss teams like Grasshopper and Servette, as well as with the Swiss national team, whom he led to the quarterfinals of the 1938 and 1954 World Cups.

3. GUSTAV SEBES

It was Sebes who molded the brilliant Hungarian teams of the '50s, and while there can be no doubting the quality of the players in the team, Sebes's tweaking of the "WM" system created tactical havoc as well. In this case, Nandor Hidegkuti, who was supposedly a center forward, dropped deep into midfield, feeding the likes of Sandor Kocsis and Ferenc Puskas. The approach created confusion in the three-man backlines of the day, especially for the center half who didn't know whether to stay with Hidegkuti and leave dangerous gaps in behind him, or let him roam freely and thus give him time and space on the ball to carve out opportunities.

4. BELA GUTTMAN

A coaching contemporary of Sebes, Guttman was also

Hungarian-born, but his nomadic coaching existence took him to the corners of the globe, never staying in one place for more than two years. Why? "The third season is fatal," said Guttman.

One of his stops included a two-year spell with Brazilian club Sao Paulo F.C., where he introduced a 4-2-4 system that had four dedicated defenders in a line. The innovation was designed to combat Hidegkuti's attacking midfield role, and was adopted by Brazilian national team head coach Vicente Feola for the 1958 World Cup. (With a near perfect balance between defense and attack, Brazil romped to their first World Cup crown.) Guttman later took his act to Portugal with Benfica, where he won two European Cups.

5. SIR ALF RAMSEY

They were called the "Wingless Wonders," that being the England side that won the 1966 World Cup, and it was Ramsey's decision to take the two wing forwards and drop them into midfield that provided the next tactical leap forward. Prior to this maneuver, wingers rarely helped out in defense, but that all changed when Ramsey took over English club side Ipswich Town in the mid-'50s. Within seven seasons, Ipswich went from being stuck in the third tier of English soccer to league champions of the First Division. Ramsey was later named England manager, and his 4-4-2 alignment, blessed with a stellar midfield containing wide players Alan Ball and Martin Peters as well as the incomparable Bobby Charlton, led England to World Cup glory on home soil.

6. HELENIO HERRERA

Herrera was not the first coach to employ *catenaccio*, but he did refine and perfect it with his Inter Milan teams of the '60s. Herrera's alignment involved four man-marking defenders and a sweeper, and the idea was to soak up pressure and then nail teams with lightning-quick counterattacks. A 1-0 win was often the only aim. It didn't make for the most entertaining soccer, but it was ruthlessly effective, as Inter won two European Cup titles during the decade as well as three Serie A crowns. In addition to his astute tactical brain, Herrera was a legendary man-manager and motivator.

7. OSVALDO ZUBELDIA
The manager of Argentine side Estudiantes during the '60s, Zubeldia heralded in a new era, although some would argue that his contributions were to the detriment of the sport. Zubeldia placed a heavy emphasis on choreographed set pieces, tactical fouling, as well as a heavy use of the offside trap. He also adopted a strategy of scouting opponents heavily as well as warming up before a match, concepts which seem obvious today but back in 1965 were unheard of. Ironically, Zubeldia is rarely mentioned among the great coaches, but one of his protégés, World Cup-winning manager Carlos Bilardo, has lauded Zubeldia as a major influence on his coaching philosophy and a big reason for his success.

8. RINUS MICHELS
The Dutch coach was the proponent of what the world would come to know as "Total Football" in which players interchanged roles on the fly, with players moving from attack to defense and back, and creating much confusion among opponents in the process. Of course, such an approach requires exceptional players both in terms of on-field awareness and technique. Fortunately for Michels, he had the

services of Johan Cruyff, both at Dutch side Ajax as well as on Holland's national team. Cruyff was the team's on-field conductor, and with him pulling the strings Ajax won three European Cup crowns. Holland was unable to duplicate that success in the World Cup, although Michels later led the national team to victory at the 1988 European Championships.

9. ARRIGO SACCHI

On the surface, there wasn't much special about Sacchi's approach, which utilized a fairly standard 4-4-2. What was different was the way his teams defended further up field, where his midfielders hunted the ball in a four-man "wolf pack." It required incredible mobility on the part of these players, but with performers like Ruud Gullit, Frank Rijkaard, and Carlo Ancelotti, the goal of midfield domination was achieved with regularity. Sacchi won Serie A and European Cup titles with Milan, and he later took Italy to within a penalty shootout of the World Cup.

10. VALERI LOBANOVSKY

Coach of the famed Dynamo Kiev teams of the '80s and '90s, as well as the Soviet Union's national team, Lobanovsky was the first soccer coach of the computer age. The Ukrainian employed a team of statisticians to record a player's every move on the field, and he used computer technology to increase the performance of his players. While some criticized Lovanovsky's approach as being sterile, there could be no arguing with his results. His teams at club level won over a dozen league titles in the Soviet and Ukrainian leagues, and he also led the Soviet Union to the final of the 1988 European Championships.

Ghosts in the Goalmouth

I t's been said that necessity is the mother of invention, and given the relatively low scoring nature of soccer, some players—and fans—have gone to extraordinary lengths to see their team get on the scoreboard. But not even these efforts can account for some of the bizarre circumstances that have led to goals being given and taken away.

1. GIVE THAT MAN A RAISE

Home cooking never tasted as good as it did during a 2006 Paulista Football Federation Cup match between Santa-cruzense and visiting Sorocaba. With Soracaba clinging to a 1-0 lead in the eighty-ninth minute, Santacruzense striker Samuel saw his attempt at goal go wide. Upon retrieving the wayward shot, a ballboy then proceeded to tap the ball into the net, and to the dismay of the Sorocaba players referee Silvia Regina de Oliveira gave a tying goal. Oliveira, who admitted later she had her back turned when the ball went in, consulted her linesman, who agreed that a goal should be given. The match finished 1-1. The soccer authorities refused to annul the result, but Oliveira, who earlier had become the first woman ever to referee a Brazilian Championship match, was suspended, as was the assistant referee.

2. **THE PHANTOM GOAL**

The scene was a 1994 Bundesliga match between Bayern Munich and Nuremberg. Bayern were attempting to win yet another championship while Nuremberg was fighting to avoid relegation. So with over 66,000 fans packing Bayern's Olympiastadion, one of the most bizarre goals in German league history occurred. A goalmouth scramble apparently came to nothing when Bayern defender Thomas Helmer, from a distance of five feet, attempted to backheel the ball into the net, but shot wide. Cue the trash-talk, with Nuremberg goalkeeper Andreas Kopke graciously inform-ing Helmer that it's, "more difficult to miss than to score!" As it turns out, the joke was on Kopke. The referee, at the behest of his assistant Jars Joblonski, ruled the ball went in even though it clearly hadn't. Bayern ended up winning the match 2-1, but the German football federation stepped in and annulled the result, forcing a replay. Nuremberg didn't get any joy in the rescheduled match either, losing 5-0. At the end of the season, Bayern were crowned champions and Nuremberg was duly relegated . . . on goal difference.

3. **CRIME AND PUNISHMENT**

"The referee had too much influence on the game," is a lament of coaches everywhere. But in the 2001 edition of England's Great Bromley Cup, such a charge might have had some merit. The game in question saw Wimpole 2000 squaring off against Earls Colne reserves. Late in the match and to the surprise of all assembled, referee Brian Savill took a cross out of the air with his hand and lashed home a splendid volley to score Wimpole's second goal of the game. Of course, the fact that his tally made the score 18-2 in favor of Earls Colne made his actions a bit more sporting than one might have otherwise thought. Enter the curmudgeons from the English Football Association, who, at the urging of the Essex Country FA, suspended Savill for seven weeks for apparently "bringing the game into disrepute." Rather than take his punishment, Savill resigned, accusing the FA of having "no sense of humor."

4. A BAD DAY AT THE OFFICE

January 21, 1995, was an ordinary day for most people, but for Germinal Ekeren defender Stan Van den Buys it was a day he set one of the most dubious records in soccer history as he managed to complete a hat trick of own goals in a match against Anderlecht. Every one of them was crucial as well, with Anderlecht prevailing 3-2.

5. DIALING LONG DISTANCE

Shooting from inside your own half is not a high percentage play, but if there were ever a player who was allowed to shoot from anywhere, it would be Roger Garcia. Not only did the Spanish midfielder score three times during his career from his own half of the field, but all of the goals came within a twelve-month period beginning in 2002. Garcia began his barrage in October 2002 while playing for Espanyol during a league match against Recreativo Huelva. Six months later, Garcia dropped his second bomb on the road against Rayo Vallecano. After moving to Villareal the following season, Garcia completed his hat trick of long distance strikes against Turkish side Galatasaray in the 2003–04 UEFA Cup.

6. LAW AND DISORDER

Former Scottish international Dennis Law enjoyed a long and storied career at club level, mostly with Manchester United. But it was while playing with Manchester City that

Law had the most prolific day of his career, only to see it erased from the record books. In 1961, City were due to play Luton Town in the fourth round of the FA Cup, and Law was in epic form, scoring an incredible six goals to stake Man City to a 6-2 lead. But a field that was already in bad shape was soon determined to be unplayable, and the match was abandoned with twenty minutes to go, meaning the entire match would have to be replayed. Law duly scored again in the rematch, but Luton emerged victorious, winning 3-1.

7. THE TWO-MAN PENALTY

Johan Cruyff was famous for a lot of things: Total Football, the "Cruyff Turn," and chain smoking. But among his more legendary feats was the infamous "two-man penalty" he uncorked with teammate Jesper Olsen while playing with Ajax in 1982. With Ajax in the midst of routing Sport Helmond, Cruyff stepped up to take a penalty kick. But instead of shooting he passed the ball to the onrushing Olsen, who then tapped it back for Cruyff to score into an empty net, amid exasperated looks from his opponents. But while Cruyff was every bit the innovator on the field, he was not the first player to be involved in such a stunt. That honor goes to Belgian international Rik Coppens, who performed the feat with teammate Andre Piters during a 1957 World Cup qualifier against Iceland.

8. THE OLYMPIC GOAL

Fresh from being crowned 1924 Olympic champions, Uruguay were invited to play Argentina in a friendly. Argentina prevailed 2-1, with the difference being a goal scored directly from corner kick by Cesareo Onzari. The feat was referred to thereafter as a "gol olímpico," and while rare it has been repeated a fair number of times. Colombian Marcos

Coll duplicated the feat in a 4-4 against the Soviet Union during the 1962 World Cup. But the man regarded as the king of the Olympic goal is former Turkish international Sukru Gulesin, who in the course of scoring 226 goals during his club career managed to score thirty-two of them directly from corners.

9. THAT'S USING YOUR HEAD

Knocking the ball out of a goalkeeper's hands is supposed to be against the rules. But that didn't stop Nottingham Forest's Gary Crosby from coming up with a unique way to dispossess the keeper. With Forest taking on Manchester City in 1990, City goalkeeper Andy Dibble was cradling the ball in one hand as he looked upfield. The quick-thinking Crosby was trailing the play, and snuck up behind Dibble, headed the ball out of his palm, and proceeded to roll the ball into an empty net. It proved to be the only goal of the game.

10. BALLOON PAYMENT

How Manchester City keep finding themselves the victim of bizarre incidents is one of the great mysteries, and supporters of the Blues were aghast to find that their penchant for weird calamities was still alive in 2008. City had traveled to Sheffield United for a fourth-round FA Cup tie, and to celebrate the occasion their fans littered the field with blue and white ballons. But in a case of karmic overload, those same balloons earned an assist on United's first goal when Lee Martin's cross deflected off two balloons, wrong-footed City defender Michael Ball, and fell invitingly for United forward Luton Shelton to score from close range. City goalkeeper Joe Hart commenced with a spree of balloon-popping, but it didn't put any more air in City's sails. They lost the game 2-1.

Goalkeeper Gaffes

One psychological ploy used on keepers is to tell them that any goal they concede is never the fault of just one person. But there have been occasions where not even a session with Dr. Phil could convince the man between the sticks that they weren't solely to blame.

1. LORD ARTHUR KINNAIRD

Kinnaird was one of the founding fathers of English soccer in the late 1800s, and in addition to being an administrator he was also one of the leading players of his day. Kinnaird played every position from goalkeeper to forward, and his participation in eight FA Cup finals, along with five triumphs, are both records. But it was during the 1877 FA Cup final that Kinnaird recorded a rather dubious achievement. Playing in goal for Wanderers against Oxford University, Kinnaird fielded an easy long distance shot, but then proceeded to gift a goal to the opposition by stepping back over the goal line. Rumor has it that Kinnaird tried to use his position on the FA Council to have the score not listed as an own goal, but it was finally recorded as such over a century later. Wanderers still won the match 2-1 in extra time.

2. ANDONI ZUBIZARRETA

Zubizarreta enjoyed a lengthy career at both club and international level, and his 622 appearances in Spain's La Liga remains a record. But one moment he has struggled to live down occurred during Spain's opening match against Nigeria at the 1998 World Cup. With Spain leading 2-1, Zubizarreta parried a cross from Nigeria's Garba Lawal into his own net. Spain eventually lost the match 3-2, and the loss proved crucial in their inability to advance out of the first round. After Spain's elimination, Zubizarreta retired from international soccer.

3. HANS-JORG BUTT

Butt was Bayer Leverkusen's designated penalty taker in 2004, a strategy that deserved a serious re-think following their league match against Schalke on April 17. Butt had just converted a penalty to put his team 3-1 up in the seventy-sixth minute, and with the game apparently safe he proceeded to go on walk-about, high-fiving every teammate in sight. Meanwhile, Schalke's quick-thinking duo of Ebbe Sand and Mike Hanke immediately took the kickoff, with Hanke lobbing the ball over Butt and into the goal from just inside the halfway line. A quick viewing of the video on YouTube makes it tough to determine what is funnier, Butt's shocked expression or his teammates laughing at him. Butt could at least joke about it afterward, as Bayer still won the match 3-2.

4. MANUEL CAMACHO

Players who can interact with the fans are always valued by the front office, but in a 1967 National Professional Soccer League match between the Baltimore Bays and the Chicago Spurs, such interpersonal skills proved to be the undoing of Camacho. It seems that just as the second half was about to begin, Camacho was chatting with some spectators, and when the whistle blew he was nowhere near his goal. That allowed alert Baltimore forward Ruben Garcete to score straight from the kickoff in a mere four seconds. Camacho undoubtedly remains high on Garcete's Christmas card list, as it was the only NPSL goal he ever scored.

5. FABIO

No, not *that* Fabio, although given the way the goalkeeper for Brazilian side Cruzeiro performed during a May 2007 match against local rivals Atletico Mineiro, the supermodel might have done better. Atletico had just scored their third goal of the game when Fabio began a belated walk back to his net to retrieve the ball. Unbeknownst to him, the match had restarted with a different ball, and when Atletico forward Vanderlei intercepted the kickoff, he proceeded to score while Fabio still had his back turned. Not only did Cruzeiro lose the match 4-0, but adding injury to insult was the fact that Fabio injured his knee in the match, an ailment that sidelined him for several months.

6. PAUL ROBINSON

It went down in the history books as a Gary Neville own goal, but that's the equivalent of a golfer blaming his five iron. In fact, a golf club might have come in handy for Robinson during England's Euro 2008 qualifying match in Croatia. England were already 1-0 down when Neville's innocuous looking back-pass hit a divot in the ground, and bounced over Robinson's foot as he attempted to clear the ball up field, and into the net. Robinson's swing and a miss resulted in a mammoth loss of confidence, and the results contributed to England missing out on the Euro 2008 finals.

7. JUERGEN SIERENS
Players are taught from an early age to play to the whistle, but that lesson was lost on Sierens during a 2005 Belgian league match between Roeselare and Charleroi. Sierens had just undergone a heavy challenge from Charleroi forward Sebastien Chabaud, and thinking a free kick had been awarded, placed the ball on the ground a few yards in front of him. At that point, Charleroi striker Francois Sterchele proceeded to tap the ball into an empty net and was awarded with a goal. "My world collapsed," Sierens was quoted as saying on uefa.com. "I woke up a few times thinking about it last night."

8. PETER ENCKELMAN
With the advent of the back-pass rule that prevents keepers from handling passes from teammates, keepers are always encouraged to work on their foot skills. Aston Villa fans will now wish Enckelman had heeded that advice. During a September 2002 English Premier League match between Aston Villa and local rivals Birmingham City, Enckelman prepared to receive a throw-in from teammate Olaf Mellberg only to see the ball roll underneath his foot and directly into the goal for Birmingham's second goal of the game. Some controversy ensued in that a goal cannot be scored directly from a throw-in, and it appeared as though Enckelman never touched the ball. But the goal was allowed to stand, and with Birmingham ultimately prevailing 3-0, Enckelman's reputation with Villa fans was forever tarnished.

9. BJARTE FLEM
The safest place for a ball is supposed to be in a goalkeeper's hands, but Flem hacked up one of the most hilarious own

goals in history during a Norwegian League match in 1988 between Tromso and Sogndal. The Tromso keeper had just collected an errant Sogndal pass and was attempting to throw the ball out to a teammate. Apparently changing his mind in mid-heave, he contrived to throw it straight into his own goal instead. The fact that the incident was shown live on Norwegian television only added to the legend. Fortunately for Flem, he managed to overcome his mistake and manned the Tromso net for a few more years.

10. RENE HIGUITA

The Colombian was well known for his dribbling forays outside of his own goal area, but Higuita received his comeuppance during Colombia's second round tilt against Cameroon at the 1990 World Cup. Daring to evade Cameroonian forward Roger Milla with the ball at his feet, Higuita was stripped clean by Milla instead, gifting Cameroon their second goal of the game and condemning Colombia to a 2-0 defeat.

Keepers Who Scored

In addition to having a well-deserved reputation for eccentricity, goalkeepers are often referred to as "the last line of defense, the first line of attack." But inside of some goalkeepers is a forward dying to get out, which explains why a select few have ventured out of their own penalty area to pop up for some vital goals. While these moves undoubtedly drove their coaches to distraction, their tallies have been treasured by their teammates.

1. JOSE CHILAVERT, VÉLEZ SÁRSFIELD AND PARAGUAY

While most keepers only get one shot at scoring, the Paraguayan international was one of the few goalkeepers known for his goal-scoring exploits. Blessed with a shot that was as powerful as his trash talking, Chilavert became Vélez's dead-ball specialist, scoring sixty-two goals, including eight in international play.

Among his most memorable tallies was a curling free kick in an international friendly against Argentina. Chilavert was also the only keeper known to have netted a hat trick, which he did in an Argentine league match against Ferro Carril Oeste.

2. **ROGERIO CENI, SAO PAULO AND BRAZIL**

While Ceni is far less known than the flamboyant Chilavert, he nevertheless surpassed the Paraguayan, tallying over seventy goals with his club Sao Paulo, most of them from free kicks.

It was on August 20, 2006, in a league match against Cruzeiro that Ceni claimed the record over Chilavert, netting twice, once on a penalty and once on a free kick. A penalty kick goal on October 29 against Mexican side Chivas saw Ceni become Sao Paulo's all-time leading scorer in the prestigious Copa Libertadores.

3. **ROBERTO BONANO, RIVER PLATE**

Bonano only has one goal on his résumé, but he'll go down in the history books alongside Chilavert, as both keepers scored penalties in a Mercosur Cup match on August 2, 2000. It marked only the second time that two keepers had scored in a top-flight match. The first occurred back in 1910 between Scottish sides Third Lanark and Motherwell, although back then the rules allowed keepers to use their hands all the way up to the halfway line.

4. **JIMMY GLASS, CARLISLE UNITED**

Goals aren't any more dramatic than the one that Glass scored on the last day of the English season in 1998 against Plymouth Argyle. Sitting at the bottom of the fourth tier of English soccer, United needed to beat Plymouth in order to avoid being relegated into the semi-professional ranks. With the score tied 1-1 and time running out, Carlisle won a corner kick, and with nothing to lose Glass ran into the opposition penalty area. The Plymouth keeper parried an initial shot, but Glass was there to pounce on the rebound, and his goal with just ten seconds left allowed United to avoid the drop.

While Glass will likely never have to buy a drink in Carlisle again, the goalkeeper was on loan from Swindon, and Carlisle opted not to sign him on a permanent basis. He bounced around the lower leagues for a few more seasons before retiring, making him truly a one-hit wonder.

5. PAT JENNINGS, TOTTENHAM HOTSPURS

Tottenham were playing Manchester United in a match called the Charity Shield, which usually pits the previous year's league champion against that season's winner of the F.A. Cup. On this occasion, a clearance from Jennings caught a gust of wind and sailed over the head of his opposite number, Alex Stepney.

6. ANDRES PALOP, SEVILLA

While Glass's heroics kept Carlisle United from being relegated, Palop went one better during the 2007 UEFA Cup. Sevilla were on the verge of being eliminated by Ukrainian side Shaktar Donetsk in the round of sixteen, when four minutes into stoppage time, Palop nodded home Daniel Alves' cross to tie the match. Sevilla then prevailed in overtime and went on to claim the tournament trophy two months later against RCD Espanyol, with Palop saving three of four shots during the penalty kick shootout.

7. HANS-JÖRG BUTT, HAMBURG SV

Butt might have been more well-known throughout the world had he not had the misfortune of playing in the same era as German legend Oliver Kahn. However, Butt did make a name for himself as a clinical penalty taker, tallying nineteen times between 1997 and 2001. Butt even led Hamburg in goals during the 2000 season, scoring nine times, something which the team's forwards did not find the least bit amusing.

8. **BRAD FRIEDEL, BLACKBURN ROVERS**

The American keeper is best remembered for his play in the 2002 World Cup, where he helped lead the United States to a quarterfinal finish. But in a 2004 English Premier League match against Charlton, and with his side trailing by a goal late in the game, the American went forward for a corner and earned his side a priceless equalizer. It turned out to be for naught, however, as Charlton's Claus Jensen scored just a minute later, negating Friedel's heroics.

9. **PAUL ROBINSON, LEEDS UNITED AND TOTTENHAM HOTSPURS**

Robinson was a hero at both ends of the field during Leeds United's Carling Cup match against Swindon Town in 2003. Trailing 2-1 deep into stoppage time, Robinson scored a stunning equalizer that pushed the match into overtime. When the game went to penalties, Robinson was the hero again, saving two spot kicks to give Leeds the victory.

Robinson added to his tally in March 2007 while suiting up for Tottenham in a league match against Watford. The Spurs' keeper launched a free kick from deep inside his own half that bounced once near the top of the Watford penalty area and over a stranded Ben Foster in the Watford goal. Tottenham won the match 3-1.

10. **PETER SCHMEICHEL, MANCHESTER UNITED, ASTON VILLA, AND DENMARK**

Perhaps the best goalkeeper of the '90s, the hulking Schmeichel was known to venture forward during desperate times. After scoring a total of eight goals for Danish sides Hvidovre IF and Brondby IF, Schmeichel moved to English giants Manchester United, where he once scored on a header in a 1995 UEFA Cup match against Rotor

Volgograd. The goal allowed United to tie the match 3-3, but his side went out on the away goals rule. Schmeichel also tallied the first goal by a goalkeeper in the history of the English Premier League (which began play in 1991), when he scored for Aston Villa on October 20, 2001, in a 3-2 defeat to Everton.

Emergency Keepers

The phrase, "So easy, even a caveman can do it," does not apply to goalkeepers, but there have been occasions when outfield players have been forced to don the gloves and deputize in goal. And a select few have performed splendidly during their short stints between the sticks.

1. NAT LOFTHOUSE
A prolific forward who made thirty-three appearances for England, Lofthouse found out what life was like on the other side during a February 1957 league match between Lofthouse's Bolton Wanderers and opponents Wolverhampton Wanderers. Already down 3-0 at halftime, Bolton lost goalkeeper Eddie Hopkinson to a hand injury, and since substitutes weren't allowed in those days, it was left to Lofthouse to replace him. What followed was a spirited fight-back that saw Bolton score two goals and Lofthouse save a penalty, but it wasn't enough as Wolves won 3-2.

2. NIALL QUINN
The Irish international's memories in goal are a bit happier.

Quinn had already scored for club side Manchester City in a 1991 league match against Derby County when nominal keeper Tony Coton went down injured. Goalkeepers were rarely among the list of eligible subs back then, so it was up to Quinn to take up residence between the sticks. As luck would have it, Derby won a penalty, but Quinn was equal to the task, saving Dean Saunders' attempt and helping City to a 2-1 victory.

Quinn went on to reprise his goalkeeping exploits eight years later. Suiting up for Sunderland, a Quinn goal put the Wearsiders up 1-0. But when goalkeeper Thomas Sorenson was injured Quinn came to the rescue yet again for the game's last fourteen minutes, keeping a clean sheet in the process.

3. ERIC VISCAAL
Viscaal equaled Quinn's heroics, but in slightly different circumstances. During a Belgium league match between Viscaal's AA Ghent and Lokeren in 1994, Viscaal was forced to take over in goal after Ghent's regular keeper had been sent off. Viscaal saved the ensuing penalty to keep his team in the match. When Ghent won a penalty late in the match, up strode Viscaal and duly slotted home the equalizer.

4. DAVID WEBB
The Englishman made his living primarily as a defender, but during the 1971–72 season Webb filled in for an injured Peter Bonetti during a 1-1 draw with Coventry. With Chelsea's first-choice keepers still injured the following week, Webb went in goal again and earned the shutout in a 2-0 victory.

5. MIA HAMM
The world's most famous female player survived a memo-

rable stint in goal during a 1995 World Cup match against Denmark. Nominal goalkeeper Brianna Scurry was sent off late in the match, and with the United States out of substitutes Hamm was forced to stand in. Hamm proved herself a pretty fair understudy, recording two saves in five shutout minutes to preserve a 2-0 victory. She remains the only outfield player to tend goal in a Women's World Cup.

6. NEIL MCBAIN

If ever there was an emergency that deserved a 911 call, the situation facing McBain definitely qualified. In 1947, the New Brighton manager was faced with a severe player shortage that left him without a goalkeeper for the match against Hartlepool United. So McBain, a midfielder during his playing days, resorted to putting himself in goal. New Brighton lost the match 3-0, but McBain, then fifty-two years old, became the oldest player to play in an English league match.

7. MICHAEL TARNAT

Bayern Munich must have thought someone put a hex on their goalkeepers during a league match against Eintracht Frankfurt during the 1999–2000 Bundesliga campaign. First, starter Oliver Kahn injured a hamstring during a collision with teammate Sammy Kuffor. Then backup Bernd Dreher was injured just ten minutes after coming on, leaving Tarnat to assume the goalkeeping duties. Bayern trailed 1-0 at the time, but a late rally saw them earn a 2-1 victory.

8. JOHN TERRY

The same bug that struck Bayern Munich hit Chelsea on October 14, 2006, when in a league match against Reading, Chelsea lost starting keeper Petr Cech to a fractured skull, and substitute Carlo Cudicini was knocked unconscious after colliding with a Reading player. Into the fray stepped Terry who managed to keep a clean sheet for the few minutes that remained in the game.

9. EMMANUEL KUFFOUR

It is rare for an outfield player to go in goal following an injury to the netminder. Rarer still is the time when that player enters the match due to poor play by the starter. But the case of Kuffor deserves a category all its own. During a 2001 World Cup qualifier Nigeria scored three goals against Ghana in the first thirty-five minutes, forcing Ghana to bring in Osei Boateng for the ineffective James Nanor. But Boateng was sent off after a mere two minutes, leaving Kuffour to take his place. As it turned out Kuffour did a better job than any of his predecessors, pitching a shutout the rest of the way, although the Black Stars still went down to defeat.

10. JAN KOLLER

The six-foot-eight Czech forward was a goalkeeper during his youth, and that training paid off during a German league match on November 9, 2002. Koller had already scored for Borussia Dortmund against Bayern Munich when teammate Jens Lehmann was sent off midway through the second half. With Dortmund out of subs, Koller was nominated as stand-in and performed so well he was named to the Bundesliga's Team of the Week as a goalkeeper. His heroics, however, weren't enough to stop Bayern from winning the match 2-1.

Super Subs

They're the players who are asked to change the course of a match, but more often than not their efforts only lead to futility. Yet there have been a select few who had a lasting impact and made their coaches look like geniuses in the process.

1. JUAN BASAGUREN

Substitutes were introduced at the World Cup in 1970, and while the USSR's Anatoli Pusatch went into the books as the first-ever replacement, it was Basaguren who became the tournament's first substitute to score a goal, notching the final tally in Mexico's 4-0 win over El Salvador.

2. LAZLO KISS

Kiss took the term "super-sub" to extremes when he came on in the second half of Hungary's match with El Salvador at the 1982 World Cup. With his side already up 5-1, Kiss went on to score a hat trick just twenty-two minutes after coming on, becoming the first, and so far only substitute to score three goals in a World Cup match. Kiss wasn't the only sub to score that day either. Teammate Lazar Szentes and El Salvador's Luis Ramirez also scored, making it the only time three subs scored in a single World Cup match. The game finished 10-1 in favor of Hungary.

3. **ALESSANDRO ALTOBELLI**
When the 1982 World Cup final dawned, Altobelli looked set to play little to no part at all in the match. But by the end of the day, the Italian forward set a trio of marks that still stand. Altobelli's first contribution came in the eighth minute when he entered the match for the injured Francesco Graziani, making it the earliest-ever substitution in a World Cup final. And with just nine minutes remaining, Altobelli became the first sub to ever score in a World Cup final, when his low drive gave Italy an insurmountable three-goal lead in what would eventually be a 3-1 victory. Altobelli was then taken off with just two minutes to go, making him the only substitute to be substituted for in a World Cup final.

4. **ROGER MILLA**
If there was ever a player worthy of the moniker of "super-sub" then Milla was it, as he was the catalyst for Cameroon's magnificent run to the quarterfinals. The former African Player of the Year came on in the second half to score two goals in the Indomitable Lions' 2-1 win over Romania in the first round, and he repeated the feat in Cameroon's second round match against Colombia, scoring both of his goals in extra time.

5. **AUSTRALIA VS. JAPAN**
A successful substitute can make a manager look good, but at the 2006 World Cup the moves Australian head coach Guus Hiddink made against Japan practically qualified him for membership in Mensa. The Socceroos were trailing 1-0 late in the match when they were bailed out by goals from

not one, but two substitutes. Two strikes in a five-minute span by Tim Cahill, the second with just a minute of normal time remaining, gave Australia an unlikely 2-1 lead. And when another sub, John Aloisi, scored two minutes into stoppage time, the Aussies' victory was made safe.

6. EBBE SAND

"He scored with his first touch!" is a phrase that nearly every soccer commentator has in his arsenal. And perhaps the closest it came to being used in a World Cup was in a 1998 second round match between Denmark and Nigeria, when Sand scored a mere sixteen seconds after coming on. Technically, Sand scored with his third touch of the ball, but never has a substitute's impact been more immediate in the World Cup.

7. KARL-HEINZ RUMMENIGGE

Substitutes are a part of any game, but rarely have the stakes been higher, or a team so desperate, as in the 1982 World Cup semifinal between West Germany and France. The Germans had just gone 2-1 down in extra time when Rummenigge, hobbled by knee problems the entire tournament, came on. Alain Giresse soon made it 3-1 for France, but Rummenigge was the catalyst for an inspired fight-back. His goal just four minutes after Giresse's gave West Germany hope, and he was involved in the buildup to Klaus Fischer's bicycle kick equalizer. Rummenigge scored in the subsequent penalty kick shootout, one in which West Germany prevailed.

8. GIUSEPPE BERGOMI

Bergomi was looking forward to a long day on the bench prior to Italy's first round matchup with Austria at the 1998

World Cup. But when Alessandro Nesta tore knee ligaments just four minutes into the match, Bergomi was inserted into the lineup and helped Italy to a 2-1 victory. The substitution equaled the earliest in World Cup history. Steve Hodge replaced England's oft-injured captain Bryan Robson after four minutes in a 1986 match against Morocco, and the mark was equaled in 2006 when England's Peter Crouch replaced an injured Michael Owen in a first round match against Sweden. Bergomi was the only member of this trio to walk off the field victorious, however.

9. LUCA MARCHEGIANI

Italy's situation was a bit more dire four years earlier. The tournament favorites had lost 1-0 to Ireland in their opening match, and when Gianluca Pagliuca became the first goalkeeper in World Cup history to be red-carded in their next match against Norway, the Italians prospects looked grim indeed. Enter Marchegiani, who was subbed in for playmaker Roberto Baggio and helped lead Italy to a priceless 1-0 victory that allowed them to advance to the second round.

10. RUDI VOELLER

An inspired substitution can't always prevent defeat, and that was the case in the 1986 World Cup final between West Germany and Argentina. The Diego Maradona-inspired Argentines went into halftime up 1-0 when Voeller entered the match. He initially did little to change West Germany's fortunes, as Jorge Valdano scored to extend Argentina's lead. But Voeller then flicked on Andreas Brehme's corner kick for Rummenigge to score at the far post, and Voeller then tied the match eight minutes later when he stabbed home another Brehme corner kick. Unfortunately, Voeller's heroics were for naught, as Jorge Burruchaga scored the winner for Argentina just three minutes later to win the match 3-2. Including the 2006 World Cup, Voeller's goal marked the second and last time a substitute scored in a World Cup final.

Most Expensive Players

Throughout soccer's history, transfer fees (the amount paid by one club to purchase a player under contract at another) have gradually edged higher and higher. But in the late 1990s and early 2000s, the transfer market reached a new level of frenzy, with tens of millions of dollars being spent on some of the biggest names in the game. Some were worth the money, while others failed to live up to their billing, but their names—not to mention their price tags—live on.

1. ZINEDINE ZIDANE

The Frenchman may be better known now for his famous head-butt on Italian defender Marco Materazzi at the 2006 World Cup, but his 2001 transfer from Italian giants Juventus to Spanish powerhouse Real Madrid for £46 million (equivalent to $66 million at the time) remains the biggest transfer fee paid. Unlike some others on this list, Zidane was worth every penny, leading Real to their ninth UEFA Champions League crown in 2002 and the La Liga title in 2003.

2. LUIS FIGO

When the Portuguese midfielder left Barcelona for Real Madrid in 2000 in a £37 million move, it was like one of the

Zidedine Zidane of Real Madrid settles the ball against Barcelona at Camp Nou, Barcelona, Spain, April 1, 2006. When Real purchased Zidane's contract from Italian giant Juventus in 2001, the transfer fee of $66 million made the Frenchman the world's most expensive player. *Brooks Parkenridge/ isiphotos.com*

Hatfields moving in with the McCoys. His return to the Nou Camp Stadium in 2002 saw a variety of objects thrown at him, including a pig's head. Figo played on, however, leading Real to the 2001 La Liga title, as well as earning the 2001 FIFA World Footballer of the Year award. He later combined with Zidane to win even more honors at Real.

3. HERNAN CRESPO

The Argentine moved from Parma to Italian rivals Lazio in June 2000 for what was then a world record transfer fee of

Thanks for the Book. I really liked it! I Love you!!

£37 million. While Crespo was an initial hit with the Roman club, leading the Serie A in scoring during the 2000–01 season with twenty-six goals, his stay in the Italian capital was short-lived. He was sold just before the 2002–03 season to Inter Milan for less than half of what Lazio had paid Parma.

4. GIANLUIGI BUFFON
The only goalkeeper to crack the top ten, Buffon's move from Parma to Juventus for £32.6 million in 2001 was thought to be madness, but the Italian international soon became a fixture with the Turin club, leading Juve to Serie A titles in 2001 and 2002. The club were famously stripped of two other titles, and relegated to Serie B for the first time in their history following a match-fixing scandal in 2006. But Buffon remained with the side, helping them earn promotion back to Serie A for the 2007–08 season.

5. ROBINHO
When Robinho indicated in the summer of 2008 that he wanted to leave Spanish champions Real Madrid, everyone assumed he would head to deep-pocketed Chelsea. But Manchester City, who had just recently been taken over by the investment company Abu Dhabi United Group, wedged their way into conversation, and ultimately won the race for the Brazilian forward's signature. The transfer fee of £32.5 million appears to be money well-spent so far, with Robinho scoring on his debut against Chelsea in September of 2008.

6. CHRISTIAN VIERI
The hulking forward has bounced around numerous clubs in his career, playing for half a dozen Serie A sides alone, but in 1999 he was part of a then world record £32 million

fee when he moved from Lazio to Inter Milan. History would prove that Inter got the best years of Vieri's career, as he hit double figures in goals during each of his five seasons with the club and led the league in scoring in 2002–03. Alas, it was not enough to lead Inter to the championship, and although they eventually won the crown in 2005–06, Vieri was long gone by then.

7. ANDIRY SHEVCHENKO

In May 2006, Chelsea acquired Shevchenko for £30.8 million, but the Ukrainian didn't come close to approaching the form he enjoyed in Italy for AC Milan, where he scored 173 goals in seven seasons and led them to the 2003 UEFA Champions League title as well as the 2004 Serie A crown. In the 2006–07 campaign, "Sheva" did manage to score fourteen goals for the Blues in all competitions, but only four of those came in league play. The following season was even worse, with Shevchenko scoring just six times in all competitions. It all added up to a scant return for such a hefty investment. Shevchenko returned to Milan in mid-2008.

8. DIMITAR BERBATOV

Berbatov's two-year stint with Tottenham Hotspur saw the Bulgarian notch a total of 45 goals in all competitions, but as the his tally grew, so did interest from Manchester United. Spurs were keen to hang on to their forward, but Berbatov's desire to play in the UEFA Champions League trumped all other concerns. In September of 2008, Tottenham reluctantly sold their star to the Red Devils for fee of £30.75 million.

9. RIO FERDINAND

The Englishman is the only defender to make the top ten,

courtesy of his 2002 move from Leeds United to Manchester United for a fee of around £29.1 million. The move broke a British transfer record, and saw him reclaim the title of the world's most expensive defender from Frenchman Lilian Thuram. West Ham United had previously sold Ferdinand to Leeds back in 2000 for over £18 million. Ferdinand has provided steady service for Man U despite an eight-month suspension in 2003 and 2004 for missing a scheduled drug test.

10. GAIZKA MENDIETA

The Basque midfielder had been the lynchpin of Valencia's run to the Champions League final in both 2000 and 2001, and when he moved to Lazio in 2002 for £28.9 million fans thought his arrival would see a repeat of their Serie A championship triumph of 2000. But it was soon evident that Mendieta's best years were behind him. He lasted only one disappointing season in Rome before being loaned out to Barcelona and then English side Middlesbrough.

Weird Transfers

Deals in the soccer transfer market are usually straightforward. A player out of contract can go wherever he or she likes. Someone who is under contract can be purchased for a (sometimes exorbitant) fee. But there have been a few transactions that you won't find illustrated in any business school handbooks; and some have been so outlandish that they might even bring a smile to the face of the world's most renowned dealmakers.

1. ZAT KNIGHT
In 1999, the England international defender was plying his trade for semi-professional Rushall Olympic when Fulham of the English Premier League acquired his rights. The fee? Thirty Adidas warm-up jackets and pants. And while that might seem a miniscule price to pay, it was actually more than Rushall counted on. Since they were playing outside the professional ranks, they weren't entitled to anything at all, but Fulham owner Mohamed Al-Fayed provided the gear as a "thank you" gift. Fulham later sold Knight to Aston Villa for a cool £3.5 million.

2. IAN WRIGHT
Wright also began his career in the non-league ranks, play-

ing for Greenwich Borough when top-tier side Crystal Palace came calling. Greenwich drove a hard bargain, parting with their striker for a set of weights. As it turned out, Wright was worth his weight in iron, gold, and platinum combined as he scored over 100 goals for Crystal Palace before being sold to Arsenal for £2.5 million.

3. TONY CASCARINO
The Irish international got his break in 1982 when English side Gillingham acquired him from Crokenhill FC for what Cascarino described as "some training equipment, tracksuits, stuff like that." Cascarino went on to score seventy-eight goals for the Gills before moving on to Millwall for a £250,000 fee.

4. KENNETH KRISTENSEN
There's no record of any player sporting a "Will work for food" sign, but Kristensen has come the closest. In 2002, Norwegian third division side Floey decided to pursue Kristensen, and his club at the time, Vindbjart, decided they wouldn't stand in his way. Their asking price turned out to be Kristensen's weight (around 170 pounds) in shrimp.
"No problem, we have enough shrimp," said Floey president Rolf Guttormsen.
The exact fee was determined at a league match between the two teams, in which Kristensen was weighed courtesy of a Vindbjart-supplied scale.

5. JOHN BARNES
The Liverpool legend was spotted in 1981 by Watford boss Graham Taylor when he was playing for non-league side Sudbury Court. Eager to sign the then seventeen-year-old, Taylor offered Sudbury a new set of uniforms, and the deed

was done. Barnes went on to score over ninety goals for the Hornets before reaching even greater heights for Liverpool, who acquired the English international for just £900,000.

6. MARIUS CIOARA

Players often complain about being treated "like a piece of meat." But in the case of Cioara, such pleas have plenty of merit. In 2006, Romanian second division side UT Arad sold Cioara to fourth division outfit Regal Hornia for fifteen kilos of sausage meat. Such was Cioara's embarrassment that he quit the game rather than play on.

"The sausage taunts all got too much," Cioara said. "They were joking I would have got more from the Germans and making sausage jokes. It was a huge insult. I have decided to go to Spain where I have got a job on a farm."

Cioara's decision left his new employers aghast.

"We are upset because we lost twice—firstly because we lost a good player and secondly because we lost our team's food for a whole week," a Hornia spokesman said.

7. CARLOS TEVEZ AND JAVIER MASCHERANO

Following the 2006 World Cup, the soccer world held its breath in anticipation of where the two Argentine internationals would end up. When the pair signed with unfashionable Premier League side West Ham United, more than a few eyebrows were raised. It turns out that the duo's former team, Corinthians, didn't own the players' registrations, and that a third party called Media Sports Investments owned the pair instead, all of which was in violation of Premier League rules. Mascherano was quickly loaned out to Liverpool, but Tevez stayed at West Ham, and his goals helped the team avoid relegation to the second tier of English soccer. West Ham ultimately were fined £5.5 million for their shenanigans, a fair trade given the nearly £30 million they would have lost had they been relegated.

8. IVANO BONETTI

Before Tevez and Mascherano, there was Bonetti whose service and image rights were held by an American company following his departure from Torino in 1995. In order for his signing with English side Grimsby to go through, $100,000 had to be raised to free him from his contract, and the club was prohibited from paying the fee themselves. Bonetti paid half the amount himself with Grimsby's fans raising the other half. Was it worth it? Bonetti remains a cult hero at the club, despite playing just one season there and netting only three goals.

9. CRISTIAN BELGRADEAN

In 2006, a number of Romanian first division clubs were interested in Belgradean, the goalkeeper for Minerul Lupeni. Included in that list was CS Jiul Petrosani, but Minerul's owner, Cornel Rasmerita, who also doubled as the mayor of Lupeni, had an interesting way of computing his player's value.

"I know our keeper is wanted by a number of top clubs but I am willing to let him go to Jiul if the club's owner makes a £110 000 investment in a gas pipe that my town needs so much," said Rasmerita. Alas, the deal was never consummated.

10. DIETMAR HAMANN

Talk about buyer's remorse: Hamann left Liverpool in 2006 and signed a contract that summer for another Premiership team, Bolton Wanderers, with his new club paying no transfer fee to obtain him. But Hamann did an about-face and expressed his desire to sign for Manchester City instead. Bolton duly complied and extracted a £400,000 fee from Manchester City for their troubles. Then-Bolton manager Sam Allardyce could barely contain his glee.

"Hamann is a history breaker," Allardyce said on the club's official website. "I am the only manager to get £400,000 for a player who has never kicked a ball for the club."

Infamous Owners

Former English forward Len Shackleton devoted an entire chapter of his autobiography to what he thought owners knew about soccer. It consisted of one blank page. Such contempt has done nothing to stop many a rich businessman from diving headlong into the soccer fray, with some neglecting to check the depth of the soccer waters first.

1. JESUS GIL Y GIL

He came, he spent, he fired coaches. That pretty much sums up the chaotic reign of Gil, who presided over Spanish side Atletico Madrid from 1987 until 2003. Determined to bring Atletico out of the shadow cast by city rivals Real Madrid, Gil spent vast sums of money, and there were occasions when it paid off. Atletico claimed the King's Cup three times under Gil, and even won a memorable "double" of both the La Liga championship and the Kings Cup in 1995–96. But Gil's legendary impulsiveness—he changed managers no fewer than forty times during his reign—led to a lack of stability, and in 2000 the club was relegated to the Spanish Second Division for the first time in over sixty years. Gil's emotions led to several suspensions as well. In 1990, he was barred from attending home matches for eighteen months after calling a French referee a homosexual. Gil also ran afoul of Spain's justice system. He served eighteen months in prison following the collapse of a building he owned that killed fifty-eight people. His financial dealings also resulted in numerous investigations, and he was convicted of fraud in 2003. Gil finally died in 2004 of a stroke, and while his career was controversial, it was also entertaining.

2. **GIGI BECALI**

The Romanian businessman, politician, and owner of Steaua Bucharest appears to be doing his best to follow Gil's lead. His New Generation – Christian Democrat Party will contest the 2009 Romanian elections, despite Becali's admitted xenophobic and homophobic views. His ownership of Steaua that began in 2003 has been no less controversial. In 2007 alone he fired four coaches, including national icon Gheorge Hagi, who just so happened to be the best man at Becali's wedding. In 2004, it was reported that Becali had commissioned a Last Supper-like painting portraying him as Jesus and the players and coach as his disciples. Despite all this, Steaua have managed to maintain their place near the top of Romanian soccer, winning two league titles under his watchful eye.

3. **THAKSIN SHINAWATRA**

If experience with boardroom intrigue is part of the job description for an owner, then Shinawatra was probably overqualified. The former Prime Minister of Thailand was ousted in a military coup in 2006, and a warrant was issued for his arrest on corruption charges. Some of his assets were frozen, but not enough to prevent him from buying EPL side

Manchester City in 2007. In February 2008, Shinawatra returned to Thailand to face the charges against him, but given his abrupt firing of popular manager Sven-Goran Eriksson at the end of the 2008 season, it seems that plenty of fans wish he had stayed there. Shinawatra sold his stake later that same year.

4. ZELJKO RAZNATOVIC

Better known as Arkan, Raznatovic made his name as the notorious leader of a Serbian paramilitary group, the Tigers, that was later accused by the war crimes tribunal at The Hague of committing atrocities during the Yugoslavian Civil War. Following the cessation of hostilities (and safely ensconced in Belgrade) Raznatovic turned his sights to soccer, taking Obilic, an otherwise obscure club in the Yugoslav second division, and turning them into a powerhouse, winning the league crown during the 1997–98 season. Obilic had considerable help, however. Several opposition players spoke of death threats they received from Raznatovic, instructing them not to score against Obilic. The presence of Tiger members at the stadium added to the intimidation. With UEFA threatening to intervene, Raznatovic stepped down from Obilic, leaving control to his wife Ceca. Raznatovic's life of crime—he was once put on Interpol's Ten Most Wanted list—finally caught up to him in January 2000 when he was assassinated in Belgrade.

5. MICHAEL ROTH

While falling short of Gil levels, the owner of Bundesliga side Nuremberg has been no slouch, burning through fifteen managers during his fourteen years at "Der Club." But Roth earned even greater fame for his outburst following a 2-1 loss to Lubeck in 2003. Roth said of his players, "I have a gun. I have a license. I would be very interested in blowing their brains out." Duly motivated, the team later won promotion to the Bundesliga.

6. MAURIZIO ZAMPARINI

The owner of Italian Serie A side Palermo is another serial sacker of coaches, and even did his best impersonation of George Steinbrenner in 2007, when with weeks remaining in the season, he fired Francesco Guidolin, promoted assistant managers Rosario Pergolizzi and Renzo Gobbo, only to fire them after three games and bring back Guidolin. But Zamparini's most memorable moment was when he threatened to cut off the testicles of his players and put them in a salad. "If there is some left after dinner I will invite you over to try it," he told the assembled media.

7. VLADIMIR ROMANOV

Like his Czarist namesake, Romanov has ruled Scottish club Hearts with an iron fist, firing head coach George Burley just eight games into 2005 for the capital crime of winning all of his matches. A parade of coaches has since passed through Hearts' doors, with results slowly diminishing. Romanov's motivational methods included a threat to sell the entire playing staff should a suitable result not be achieved the following week against Dunfermline. The team drew 1-1, and while Romanov avoided making wholesale changes, some players, including captain Stephen Pressley, were sold shortly thereafter.

8. LUCIANO GAUCCI

The owner of Italian club Perugia from 1991 to 2004, Gaucci was never far from the headlines. He once fired one of his players, Korean forward Ahn Jung Hwang, for scoring the goal that knocked Italy out of the 2002 World Cup. He later tried to sign Sweden's Hanna Ljungberg in a bid to make her the first women to play in Serie A. Then there was his signing of Al-Saadi Gaddafi, the son of Libyan strongman Muammar Gaddafi, a player whose Perugia career lasted a total of one match before he failed a drug test. Gaucci was also famous for his allegations of match-fixing. But when an arrest warrant charging Gaucci with fraud was issued in 2004, he fled Italy for the Dominican Republic where he's been ever since.

9. GEORGE REYNOLDS
Safecracking and burglary aren't exactly inspiring entries on the résumé of a prospective owner, but that didn't stop English side Darlington from welcoming Reynolds with open arms back in 1999. At first, all seemed well, with Reynolds building the team a new stadium. But when results didn't match the expenses, a financial crisis ensued with Reynolds resigning and the team being taken over by the club's creditors. Darlington survived, but Reynolds was later arrested and convicted of tax fraud.

10. DMITRY PITERMAN
Never has an owner wanted so badly to be a coach, and when Piterman bought into Spanish side Racing Santander in 2004, he thought his dream had come true. Except the Spanish soccer authorities claimed he didn't have the requisite coaching license. Not to worry, Piterman fired the current manager and installed his own puppet coach by the name of Chuchi Cos. Avoiding relegation didn't stop Racing's shareholders from running Piterman out of town; but the Ukrainian-American businessman soon bought into Alaves, another Spanish club, with even more disastrous

results. After running through four coaches, and calling his fans "drunks and subnormals," the team was relegated following the 2005–06 season. One year later, the team was taken over by creditors with Piterman forced to sell his stake.

Under Pressure

Being a head coach isn't a job for the meek, and the stresses of the vocation can cause them to do some strange things. Or have some strange things done to them.

1. IVOR BROADIS
Managers are constantly promising a club's fans that they will always act in the best interests of the club. But what Broadis did in 1949, when he was player-manager of English side Carlisle United, had fans scratching their heads. Convinced that Carlisle needed additional funds, he decided he needed to sell a player to raise the cash. So he proceeded to sell himself to Sunderland for £18,000.

2. TONI SCHUMACHER
Coaches are hired to be fired, or so the saying goes, but even Schumacher had to be surprised at the timing of his ousting as coach of German second division side Fortuna Cologne. Trailing 2-0 at halftime to Waldhof Mannheim in December 1999, Schumacher was set to give his halftime talk only to be intercepted by owner Jean Loring, who fired him on the spot. Schumacher left the stadium immediately,

leaving his assistant in charge. Loring's tactic did little to motivate the team, as they lost 5-1.

3. BOBBY GOULD
Gould needed no such prodding from management during Peterborough United's match in 2004 against Bristol City. With his team trailing 1-0, Gould dispensed with his half-time address and quit on the spot. "I can't be associated with that side," Gould explained.

4. FELIX MOURINHO
Nothing says Merry Christmas quite like a firing, but that is the fate that befell Mourinho in 1973. The manager of Portuguese side Rio Ave was in the middle of Christmas dinner with his family when he got the call from the club's president, who informed him that his services were no longer needed. In addition to casting something of a pall over the proceedings, the incident made a lasting impression on Felix's son Jose, who went to win the UEFA Champions League as manager of Porto as well as two English Premier League titles with Chelsea. "I know all about the ups and downs of football," the younger Mourinho told the *Guardian*. "I know that one day I will be sacked." Mourinho turned out to be quite a prophet. He parted ways with Chelsea less than a year later.

5. MANUEL JOSE
The coach of Egyptian side Al-Alhy was watching his side cruise to a 4-0 league victory over Haras el-Hadoud when Jose took issue with a booking issued to defender Anis Boujelbene. But apparently Jose never took his mother's advice to use big words when expressing his feelings. He disrobed instead, and was immediately ejected. "I forgot at

that moment that I was in a country whose traditions are a little bit different than my country," said the Portuguese-born Jose. Just a *little* bit different?

6. HARRY REDKNAPP

There has been many a coach who would love nothing better than for a hypercritical fan (or journalist) to put their money where their mouth was. But in a 1994 preseason friendly between West Ham United and minor league outfit Oxford City, West Ham's then-assistant manager Redknapp struck a blow for coaches everywhere when he did just that. Annoyed at the abuse his team was taking from West Ham fan Steve Davies, Redknapp challenged him to do better, and minutes later he put Davies into the game. Redknapp later told the *Guardian,* "[Davies] ran on to the pitch and a journalist from the local Oxford paper sidled up and asked, 'Who's that Harry?' I said, 'What? Haven't you been watching the World Cup? That's the great Bulgarian Tittyshev!' The fella wasn't bad—actually, he scored!"

7. RUDI GUTENDORF

Job security isn't a trait endemic to coaching, but Gutendorf has taken this to extremes. The German-born coach managed no fewer than seventeen national teams during his fifty-plus years in coaching, including Chile and Bolivia as well as Antigua. He also managed over twenty clubs, making him soccer's resident nomad.

8. LEROY ROSENIOR

Results, or the lack of them, are usually the reason for a coach getting fired, which explains Rosenior's exasperation in May 2007. On May 17, Rosenior was unveiled as the new manager of Torquay United, who had just been relegated to England's minor leagues. A scant ten minutes after completing the press conference and the requisite interviews, Torquay owner Mike Bateson informed Rosenior that he had just sold the club, and that the new owners would probably be bringing in a new manager. It left Rosenior with one of the shortest tenures in managerial history.

9. VITTORIO POZZO

"Win or else," is a missive that has come from many an owner. But when the instruction is turned into "Win or die," and the person delivering is Italian dictator Benito Mussolini, it tends to come attached with a bit more pressure. Such were the circumstances that Pozzo worked under as Italy prepared to host the 1934 World Cup. Fortunately for the coach, Mussolini's threat was never put to the test, as Italy prevailed in the tournament, winning their first ever World Cup title.

10. MICK WADSWORTH

In January 2003, Wadsworth revealed some negotiating skills that only Donald Trump could appreciate. On his way out as boss of English side Huddersfield, Wadsworth and team chairman David Taylor managed to agree on a severance fee. As it turned out, the Huddersfield board was unable to come up with the funds, leading to a situation where, as Taylor put it, "we could not afford to sack him." The reprieve proved short-lived, as Wadsworth was fired for good two months later.

Not So Happy Families

Soccer teams are often like families. Some are like the Huxtables. Others are like the Osbournes. And then there are those who bear a closer resemblance to the Sopranos.

1. DAVID BECKHAM AND SIR ALEX FERGUSON, MANCHESTER UNITED

Ferguson, the legendary United manager, is a difficult man to please in the best of times, and the aftermath of a 2-0 loss to bitter rivals Arsenal in the 2003 FA Cup certainly didn't qualify as such. In the midst of giving his team a verbal dressing down, Ferguson kicked a soccer cleat in frustration, and it struck Beckham in the face, resulting in a cut above the eye.

"It was a freakish incident," said Ferguson. "If I tried it a hundred or a million times, it couldn't happen again. If I could, I would have carried on playing!"

But the relationship between player and coach, already strained due to Beckham's celebrity status, never recovered, and Beckham was sold to Real Madrid at the end of the season.

2. ROY KEANE AND MICK MCCARTHY, IRELAND

Prior to the 2002 World Cup, the conventional wisdom had it that Ireland would go as far as their inspirational captain Keane would carry them. But during the team's training camp on the Pacific island of Saipan, Keane became incensed at what he deemed the poor quality of the team's accommodations, and left the camp in disgust.

At McCarthy's urging, Keane returned, but when Keane made the incident public in an interview with the *Irish Times*, McCarthy felt he had no choice but to send Keane home. Opinion back in Ireland was split over the affair, but Ireland carried on and managed to progress to the second round of the tournament before falling to Spain in a penalty shootout.

3. RUUD GULLIT AND DICK ADVOCAAT, THE NETHERLANDS

When Gullit walked out of the Dutch side prior to the 1994 World Cup, it wasn't over anything as urbane as accommodations, nor was it the petty jealousies that have long undermined Holland's international efforts. It all came down to what players and coaches have been arguing about for more than a century: tactics. In this case, Gullit thought that playing a 3-4-3 system would be tactical suicide in the heat of the American summer. Advocaat disagreed.

Gullit had already walked out on the team once before, when Advocaat had the audacity to substitute him against England. The coach managed to convince his tempestuous star to return, but when he objected to Advocaat's game plan, he walked out in a huff. Gullit never played for Holland again.

4. KIERON DYER AND LEE BOWYER, NEWCASTLE UNITED

Over the course of a season, spats between teammates are as inevitable as trash talking on *The Jerry Springer Show*.

Usually they take place during practice or in the sanctity of the locker room. But in an April 2, 2005, match between English Premier League sides Aston Villa and Newcastle United, Newcastle teammates Kieron Dyer and Lee Bowyer had a set-to in the most public of forums, that being Newcastle's own St. James' Park in front of 52,000 fans.

With United having just gone behind 3-0, Bowyer had made a run down the right wing, asked Dyer for the ball, and when no pass came, unleashed a verbal tirade on his teammate. When Dyer took offense the duo exchanged blows and were duly sent off by referee Barry Knight. Bowyer was not only suspended for four games by the league, but he was viewed as the aggressor by team management and was fined over $600,000 for his part in the fracas. Dyer was hit with a three-match ban.

5. LOTHAR MATTHÄUS AND JURGEN KLINSMANN, BAYERN MUNICH AND GERMANY

At Bayern during the mid-nineties, the atmosphere in the locker room was so fraught with infighting and gossip that the club became known as "FC Hollywood." At issue was the personal rivalry between Matthäus and Klinsmann. Klinsmann succeeded Matthäus as captain of the German national team, with Matthäus accusing Klinsmann of undermining his position so that Klinsmann could take the position for himself. It was a decision that head coach Berti Vogts described as "the best I ever made." Klinsmann led Germany to the 1996 European championship while Matthäus was left off the squad and forced to watch from home.

Matthäus later bet a Bayern executive that Klinsmann would not score fifteen league goals during the 1996–97 season. (Klinsmann would go on to score exactly fifteen.)

But through it all, Bayern managed to enjoy a modicum of success. They won the 1996 UEFA Cup as well as the 1996–97 Bundesliga title.

6. JOEY BARTON AND MANCHESTER CITY

Shenanigans at company Christmas parties are nothing new. Reputations, if not jobs, have been savaged by unseemly behavior. But nothing could have prepared the employees of Manchester City for what happened at their annual shindig just prior to the Yuletide of 2004. Drunk and annoyed with youth player Jamie Tandy after Tandy tried to set fire to Barton's shirt, Barton proceeded to stick a lit cigar into Tandy's eye. Tandy was not seriously injured, but Barton was fined six weeks' wages for this indiscretion. Barton's infamy has only grown since then. In 2007 he was fined £100,000 for an assault of teammate Ousmane Dabo during training, effectively ending his time in Manchester. After being transferred to Newcastle United, Barton was convicted of assault in May 2008 and was given a six-month prison term.

7. CLINT MATHIS AND EWALD LIENEN, HANNOVER 96

When Mathis arrived in Germany in 2004, he was an immediate hit, scoring four goals in his first five matches. The next season saw Mathis and the team suffer a loss of form, resulting in the firing of head coach Ralf Ragnick. Taking his place was the conservative Ewald Lienen, and it became apparent that Mathis was falling out of favor.

In a September 25, 2005, match against Schalke 04, Lienen sent Mathis in as a late substitute, and just ninety seconds later Mathis scored with a thumping volley for the only goal of the match. Not content with scoring the game-winner, Mathis ran to Lienen on the sidelines, conspicuously tapping his wrist, indicating that the coach should have sent him on much sooner. In the age of NFL player Terrell Owens, Mathis's gesture might have seemed insignificant, but in Germany it caused an uproar, and Mathis soon not only found himself out of the lineup but heading back to the United States.

8. EYAL BERKOVIC AND JOHN HARTSON, WEST HAM UNITED

This was a bust-up that took place where they normally happen—on the practice field—and would have gone unnoticed, except for the amateur cameraman that happened to be filming practice that day back in September 1998. In this case, a heavy challenge saw Berkovic lash out at Hartson, only for the Welshman to unleash a full-blooded kick to Berkovic's jaw that would have made Bruce Lee proud. The videotape of the incident was soon everywhere.

"If my head had been a ball, it would have been in the top corner of the net," Berkovic recalled.

Hartson later made his peace with Berkovic, but that didn't stop West Ham from fining him two weeks wages—around £10,000. He was later fined an additional £20,000 by the English Football Association and suspended for three games, this after having been sold by West Ham to Wimbledon.

9. STEVE SAMPSON AND WELL, EVERYBODY, USA

After Sampson, then the U.S. interim head coach, led the team to the semifinals of the 1995 Copa America, he was given the job full-time, and the players were universal in their praise for the former collegiate coach, who had loosened the reigns on his charges and allowed them to take more initiative in attack.

By the time the 1998 World Cup arrived, Sampson's

honeymoon had long since ended. Sampson first drew the ire of veteran players when he sensationally booted captain John Harkes off the team in a disagreement over team tactics, as well as Harkes' role in the side. Sampson further ruffled feathers when he brought in several players prior to the World Cup who had taken little part in qualifying. And when the Americans proceeded to lose all three games at the finals in France, the team imploded, bashing Sampson in the press on numerous occasions.

As Harkes later noted, "The more [Sampson] coached, the worse we got." Sampson resigned just days after the United States was eliminated.

10. STEFAN EFFENBERG AND GERMANY

Effenberg was a player who possessed remarkable skill, uncanny vision, and no tact. While his charismatic leadership helped Bayern Munich win the 2001 Champions League title, he will be best remembered for his actions during a 1994 World Cup match against South Korea. With the German fans whistling at their team for their lackluster play, Effenberg made an obscene gesture at his own supporters and was sent home by coach Berti Vogts immediately following the match. It would be four years before Effenberg would suit up for the national team again.

Divided Loyalties

A rticle 18 of the FIFA code seems a fairly straightforward way of governing international eligibility. It states that only players who are citizens can suit up for their national teams, and once they do so in a FIFA sanctioned competition, they are bound to that team for life. But things weren't always so simple, and there was a time when changing countries was as easy as changing socks. Even now, deciding what team to play for can be problematic. A player's parents can hail from different countries, or he can be born in one nation while his parents are citizens of another. Or he can become a naturalized citizen after having settled in a particular nation. All of this has made determining where a player's loyalties lie more difficult than it seems.

1. LUISITO MONTI

They were called the "Oriundi," players of Italian heritage who were born elsewhere but returned to play in Italy, and in the '30s several of these players made their mark in Italian soccer, with Monti among the most celebrated.

Nicknamed "Doble Ancho" (double wide) for the ground he covered as well his ferocious tackling, Monti was born in

Argentina and helped lead them to a runner-up finish in the inaugural World Cup in 1930. But Monti's aggressive style made him plenty of enemies, and the death threats he received before the final resulted in a subdued performance. Eager to leave his homeland, Monti signed with Italian club Juventus whom he helped win several league titles, and with Italy hosting the 1934 World Cup he was quickly drafted into the national side by manager Vittorio Pozzo. There he continued his twin roles of midfield destroyer and playmaker, and helped Italy to their first world title. He remains the only player to have played in two World Cup finals for two different countries.

2. TERRY MANCINI

As much as we would like to believe that love of country is at the core of every international player, the story of Mancini shows just how unpredictable it can sometimes be. Born in London as Terry Sealy, Mancini's Irish father passed away when he was seven, and his mother soon reverted to the name Mancini.

As Mancini rose through the professional ranks, a chance conversation with club teammate Don Givens revealed that Mancini was eligible to play for Ireland due to his parentage, and on October 10, 1981, Mancini found himself lining up for the Irish in a World Cup qualifier against Poland. As the first national anthem was being played Mancini remarked to Givens, "Their anthem does go on a bit," to which Givens responded, "Be quiet. It's ours."

Mancini only appeared for Ireland five times, but did manage to score a goal against Brazil at Rio's famed Maracana Stadium.

3. **JOSE ALTAFINI**

The move from one country to another doesn't always work as well as it did for Monti. Witness the progression of Altafini, who was known as Mazola during the early part of his career in Brazil. During the 1958 World Cup, it was the nineteen-year-old Altafini, not the younger Pelé, who was in Brazil's starting lineup. And while the later stages of the tournament saw Altafini relegated to the bench at the expense of Pelé and Vava, he still walked away with a World Cup-winner's medal.

At that point Altafini engineered a move to Italian side AC Milan, and his exploits for the Rossoneri eventually won him a call-up to the Italian national team. Altafini accepted, but the 1962 tournament didn't end happily for either the player or the team as Italy was eliminated in the first round.

4. **CLARENCE SEEDORF**

If you comprised a list of great players from the former Dutch colony of Suriname, you would come up with a pretty fair starting eleven that would include Edgar Davids, Aron Winter, and Jimmy Floyd Hasselbaink. That side would be even deeper if you included Dutch players of Surinamese descent like Ruud Gullit and Frank Rijkaard. Unfortunately for Suriname, political instability led many citizens to flee for Holland during the '80s and '90s, with the Dutch national team benefiting as a result. Of the Suriname-born players who have graced Holland's national team, Seedorf is perhaps the most accomplished, having won four UEFA Champions League crowns with such high-profile clubs as Ajax, Real Madrid, and AC Milan.

At international level, Seedorf's form with Holland has been more mixed, and his feuds with various managers have seen him omitted from several tournaments. But Seedorf was around for Holland's best World Cup finish in recent years when they reached the semifinals of the 1998 World Cup.

5. MIROSLAV KLOSE

Every so often, an intense tug-of-war ensues over a player with dual nationality, and back in 2001 such a battle ensued over Klose. Born in the Polish town of Opole, Klose's family escaped the Soviet-dominated country in 1981, with the German roots of Klose's father allowing them to settle in West Germany.

When Klose established himself in the Bundesliga during the 2000–01 season, Polish head coach Jerzy Engel soon came calling, but Klose cast his lot with Germany, and the move proved telling for both countries. Klose tallied five times in both the 2002 and 2006 World Cups, becoming the only player in history to reach that mark in consecutive tournaments. Polish fans can only wonder how their country would have done with such a marksman in their side, and the issue came to a head at the 2006 World Cup when Germany prevailed over Poland 1-0 during the group phase.

6. EMMANUEL OLISADEBE

Denied by Klose, Engel soon hit upon a backup plan. In 2001, with the blessing of the Polish Football Association Engel fast-tracked the Polish citizenship of Olisadebe, a Nigerian who had been banging in the goals at league level for Polonia Warsaw.

Engel could not have been more desperate. Prior to Olisadebe being granted citizenship, Poland had failed to score in ten consecutive matches. But once the Nigerian was in the lineup, he went on a tear, scoring eight goals in qualifying for the 2002 World Cup, leading Poland to their first finals appearance in sixteen years.

7. FERENC PUSKAS

A member of Hungary's celebrated 1954 team, Puskas might very well have played in his homeland forever, but following the failed Hungarian Revolution of 1956, Puskas and many of his teammates fled the country. Back then, players were wedded to their teams for life unless they were sold, and Puskas's failure to return to his club resulted in an FFA-imposed ban of two years. But Puskas endured, signing with Real Madrid in 1958, where he led them to league and European Cup glory. And when his adopted country of Spain requested his services prior to the 1962 World Cup, Puskas duly complied.

Alas, Puskas failed to score at that tournament as Spain was eliminated in the group stage, finishing last in their pool. But Puskas's performance made him one of the few players to have played in the World Cup finals for two different countries.

8. JUAN SANTAMARIA

One of the most accomplished defenders of his day, Santamaria was born in Uruguay in 1929, and his exploits with club side Nacional saw him become an established international at the tender age of twenty-three. Santamaria was even considered two years earlier for the World Cup-winning side of 1950, but a disagreement between his club and the national team over his preferred position saw him omitted. But Santamaria made his mark four years later, starring for a Uruguayan team that reached the semifinals. It was at that tournament that Santamaria caught the eye of Real Madrid, and the Uruguayan quickly moved to Spain when Real was at their height. Like his club teammate Puskas, Santamaria was also drafted into the Spanish squad for the 1962 World Cup, but Spain's failure to get out of the first round proved a bitter pill. Santamaria did no better as Spain's head coach at the 1982 World Cup, but is still one of over fifty World Cup players who later participated as head coaches.

9. ROBERT PROSINECKI

One of the most technically gifted players of his day, Prosinecki was born in West Germany to Yugoslavian parents, making him another player with options regarding who to represent at international level. And when he debuted for Yugoslavia in 1989, he probably thought that was the end of the matter. But the Yugoslavian Civil War in the late '90s changed all that, and when Croatia gained its independence Prosinecki opted to change his international allegiance.

Having represented Yugoslavia at the 1990 World Cup, Prosinecki proved to be just as important for Croatia eight years later, helping the World Cup debutantes to a surprising third place finish. Prosinecki also remains the only player in finals history to have scored goals for two different countries, having tallied once in 1990 and three times in 1998.

10. LADISLAV KUBALA

If there was ever an international player with an identity crisis, it was Kubala, who suited up for three different countries in his international career. Born in Budapest to a Hungarian mother and Slovak father, Kubala first donned the jersey of Czechoslovakia, where he had moved in 1946 supposedly to avoid military service. When the Czechoslovakian military also tried to draft him, Kubala skipped town once again, joining Hungarian side Vasas and making his international debut for Hungary in 1948.

When Hungary was taken over by the communists, Kubala fled once more, this time to Italy before finally landing in Spain, where he became a goal-scoring legend for Barcelona. That led to an international call-up by his adopted country, for which he appeared nineteen times. Unfortunately, an injury just before the 1962 World Cup prevented Kubala from taking part. Still, Kubala's odyssey ranks as one of the more peculiar chapters in international soccer.

Bizarre Bookings

The list of bookable offenses is supposedly spelled out in Law XII in FIFA's Laws of the Game. But not even the sages in Zurich could have predicted some of the scenarios referees would eventually face.

1. CLEBERSON
When is a kiss not just a kiss? The Cabofriense defender found that out in a 2007 match against Botafogo. Cleberson had just committed a foul and appeared to be engaged in a friendly chat with referee Ubiraci Damasio, when he suddenly planted a kiss on Damasio's cheek. The referee immediately issued Cleberson a yellow card and said, "You can't kiss me." Cleberson later added, "I didn't know it was against the rules," an exchange that adolescent boys the world over could appreciate.

2. MIKE PETKE
If kissing a referee warrants a yellow card, then what sanction would kissing the ball merit? American defender Petke found out the hard way in an August 11, 1999, match between the MetroStars and D.C. United. Petke had just fouled United's Jaime Moreno, then promptly picked up the ball

and kissed it, which earned him a straight red card from referee Michael Kennedy.

3. PABLO SALINAS

Kissing is one thing, but what Salinas, forward for Bolivian side The Strongest, did seems pale by comparison. Salinas had just scored in an August 2007 Bolivian league match against bitter rivals Bolivar, when he pulled a Spiderman mask out of his shorts and put it on. While it's unclear if Salinas can do everything that a spider can, the move earned Salinas his second yellow card of the match for unsporting behavior, and he was subsequently sent off. The Strongest still ended up winning 2-0.

4. RAMIRO CORRALES

Waving a white towel is usually a sign of surrender, but in this case, it earned Corrales an ejection. The San Jose Earthquakes defender had been substituted earlier in a 2004 match against the MetroStars, when opposing midfielder Amado Guevara attempted to take a quick throw-in near the Earthquakes bench. Corrales held Guevara up, and then gently snapped the towel against his midsection, at which point Guevara promptly went down in a heap clutching his *face.* Corrales was issued a straight red while Guevara was issued a caution for diving.

5. REAL BETIS BALL BOYS

In 2006, the Spanish club side was clinging to a 1-0 lead in a home match against Atletico Madrid, when the Atletico players began to complain that the ball boys weren't returning the ball to them. The referee, one Miguel Ángel Ayza Gámez, agreed that Real's little helpers (allegedly instructed by club officials) were engaging in too much home cooking and sent them to their rooms without any supper by red carding all fourteen of them.

6. ANDY MCLAREN

The Three Strikes and You're Out Law has yet to cross the Atlantic, which is a good thing for Dundee's McLaren who earned the dubious distinction of earning three red cards in a single game. The mayhem took place in a Scottish First Division match between Dundee and Clyde. Clyde was up 2-0 when Dundee converted a penalty, at which point the fun began. McLaren was first booked for wrestling for the ball with Clyde goalkeeper David Hutton. But McLaren then punched opposition defender Eddie Malone and was sent off. Not content with a mere ejection, McLaren also struck Michael McGowan on his way to the dressing room, and although the referee didn't see it, the linesman alerted him. Called into the referee's dressing room afterward, McLaren was informed of his second red card, at which point he achieved his dubious hat trick when he kicked a hole in the door. The club released McLaren a week later.

7. ZEQUINHA

How to make a red card disappear isn't a staple of most magic acts, but that didn't stop the Portuguese youth international during the quarterfinals of the 2007 FIFA U-20 World Cup. With teammate Mano about to be ejected from the match against Chile, Zequinha attempted to intervene, by stealing the referee's red card right out of his hand. Not only did Zequinha's antics simply delay the inevitable, but they resulted in his own expulsion as well. Portugal lost the match 1-0.

8. ALEX FRANK

It's one thing to earn a red card. It's quite another to lose your team the game, which is exactly what happened to the unfortunate Frank during an Iowa high school playoff game involving Waterloo West High and Dubuque Senior. With Waterloo leading 2-1, a catchable cross was fumbled over the end line by Frank, resulting in a corner kick. Frank then uttered an expletive at himself that was within earshot of the referee, who issued the Waterloo West keeper a straight red card. As if that wasn't bad enough, Iowa high school rules dictate that a team is eliminated from the postseason if they accumulate four red cards during the season. As this was the team's fourth expulsion of the year, the game was immediately forfeited. Waterloo West athletic director Jeff Frost admirably took the high road afterwards. "It's a tough way to go out, but the rules are the rules."

9. JOHN MOORE
So when does the statute of limitations run out on fouls? Not soon enough for Hong Kong international Moore, who in a World Cup qualifying match against Palestine was booked for a tackle in the eighty-fifth minute, and then shown a second yellow card for an altercation that occurred ten minutes earlier. "I have never heard of such a decision in all the years I have been playing," Moore said.

10. ANDY WAIN
Referees have booked players on the field. They've cautioned them on the bench. But the red card that referee Wain issued in an English Sunday League match between Peterborough North End and Royal Mail AYL was one for the history books. He issued it to himself. The incident occurred after Royal Mail had scored to go up 2-1, a goal that Peterborough goalkeeper Richard McGaffin protested furiously.

But rather than ignore it, Wain threw down his whistle and appeared ready to engage in some fisticuffs with the player. Wain ultimately came to his senses, but it was enough for him to abandon the match. "It was totally unprofessional," Wain told the *BBC*. "If a player did that I would send him off, so I had to go."

Busted

The "Just Say No to Drugs" campaign has been as effective with soccer players as it has been with the public at large, which is to say it's had little impact at all. Not only have some of the most famous players in the game succumbed to the lure of illicit substances, but the performance enhancing variety has induced their share of suspensions as well.

1. DIEGO MARADONA

Argentina's talismanic midfielder has the dubious distinction of being suspended not once, but twice, for drug use. In 1991, while playing for Napoli in Italy, Maradona received a fifteen-month ban after testing positive for cocaine, an addiction that he would battle for much of his adult life. Following his suspension, Maradona bounced around several clubs, including Spanish club Sevilla as well as Argentine side Newell's Old Boys.

This was quickly followed by his return to the Argentine national team late in 1993, where he helped the Albiceleste qualify for the 1994 World Cup. That summer, Maradona was in inspirational form, scoring a memorable goal against Greece, but the party came to an abrupt halt.

Maradona tested positive for the stimulant ephedrine, and the effect on the psyche of both team and player was near-immediate. Argentina fell in the second round to Romania 3-2. As for Maradona, the expulsion signaled the end to his once glorious career.

2. WILLIE JOHNSTON

With the Scotland team already reeling from a shocking 3-1 defeat to Peru in their 1978 World Cup opener, the Scottish winger heaped further misery on the fans back home when he was thrown out of the Cup for taking a banned stimulant. Johnston claimed he was taking an over-the-counter medication for hay fever, although the reality was that he took two Reactivan tablets that are used to "increase mental alertness."

Scotland's woeful form on the field, that included a 1-1 draw with Iran, overshadowed much of the furor over his suspension, but not enough to prevent the Scottish Football Association from slapping Johnston with a lifetime international ban.

3. ERNEST JEAN-JOSEPH

With the advent of drug testing at the 1966 World Cup, Jean-Joseph became an unwitting footnote in soccer history, when in 1974 he was the first player ever to test positive at a World Cup finals. Jean-Joseph tested positive for a banned substance following Haiti's 3-1 loss to Italy. Exactly what caused Jean-Joseph's ouster isn't known, but Jean-Joseph was reportedly beaten by members of his own delegation before being sent home. A German attaché tried to intervene and was dismissed from his post for his troubles. Jean-Joseph was only suspended for the remainder of the tournament and went on to represent Haiti in later years.

His career also took him to the United States, where in 1978 he played for the Chicago Sting of the old North American Soccer League.

4. ADRIAN MUTU

In October 2004, the Romanian international was already on the outs with then-Chelsea manager Jose Mourinho when Mutu played in a World Cup qualifier against Mourinho's wishes. But whatever chance Mutu had of getting back into the squad vanished when he tested positive for cocaine, and in the midst of his seven-month worldwide ban he was sold to Juventus for a fraction of what he cost.

Mutu's journey had a happy ending, at least for him personally. In the 2005–06 season, he helped Juventus win the Serie A title that was subsequently forfeited due to a match-fixing scandal. He moved on to fellow Serie A side Fiorentina, where he has established himself as one of the best strikers in the league, and his fine form has seen him named vice-captain (no pun intended) of the Romanian national team.

5. CHRISTOPH DAUM

Just call it "Daum and Daum-er." The German coach proved that not only are managers just as susceptible as players to drugs, but they can be just as stupid as well. After a successful coaching career with German clubs such as FC Cologne and Bayer Leverkusen, Daum was set to take charge of the German national team in 2001. But when allegations of drug use surfaced in October 2000, Daum's response was "Test me." The German Federation duly called his bluff, and when an analysis of his hair came back positive for drugs, the bureaucrats at the DFB dissolved their agreement faster than you can say "breach of contract."

Daum later resurfaced in Turkey with Besiktas and Fenerbahce, and it wasn't until 2006 that he finally returned to FC Cologne, the club where he began his coaching career.

6. JUVENTUS

The Juventus teams of the mid-'90s won just about every trophy in their path: three Italian league titles as well as the 1996 UEFA Champions League. According to the team's many critics, had there been a trophy for "Contributions to Sports Medicine" Juve would have won that too.

Following accusations by rival coach Zdenek Zeman of systematic doping in 1998, a raid on Juve's training facility revealed 281 kinds of drugs, including five banned anti-inflammatory medications. Testifying at the subsequent trial of Juve chief administrator Antonio Giraudo and team doctor Riccardo Agricola for sporting fraud, Gianmartino Benzi, professor of Pharmacology at Pravia University, stated that the stocks "resembled quantities found in a small hospital." Ultimately, Juve escaped punishment. Giraudo was acquitted, while Agrilcola's initial conviction for administering EPO was later overturned. That hasn't stopped a cloud, however faint, from hanging over one of the more successful periods in Juve's history.

7. EDGAR DAVIDS

As if Juventus's critics needed any more proof, there was the suspension of their Dutch midfielder in 2001. Davids tested positive for the steroid nandrolone and was suspended for five months. The suspension was eventually reduced to four months despite his hilarious contention that homeopathic medicines were to blame for his results.

The suspension had relatively little impact on Davids' career. He went on to play three more seasons for Juve before moving on to such other highly regarded clubs as Barcelona, Inter Milan, and Ajax.

7. RIO FERDINAND
So how does a player fail a drug test without even taking one? Simple, he fails to show up, which is exactly what happened to Ferdinand in 2003. The Manchester United defender claimed he was moving into a new house on the day the test was to take place and simply forgot it had been scheduled. To some, that qualified as the pharmacological equivalent of "the dog ate my homework," and while he subsequently took—and passed—a test 36 hours later, the damage was done. The English Football Association slapped Ferdinand with an eight-month, worldwide ban that caused him to miss the rest of the 2003–04 club season as well as the European Championships in the summer of 2004. And while some thought the penalty harsh, it could have been worse, as the English FA could have handed down a two-year ban.

8. ROMARIO
Bald may be beautiful, but it was Romario's fight against baldness that earned him a suspension in 2007, when he tested positive for the stimulant finasteride. Romario claimed that the positive test was due to a hair tonic that contained the banned substance, and that he was not using it to mask the use of performance enhancing drugs. Romario's claim was viewed as a bald-faced lie, and the Brazilian Football Federation suspended him for 120 days.

9. SALVADOR CARMONA
Carmona first drew the ire of FIFA in 2005 when he tested positive for stanozolol at the 2005 Confederations Cup, just two days after a historic 1-0 win over Brazil. The problem

was the test he flunked came two days before the team departed for the tournament, causing all kinds of problems for the Mexican federation who were fined and had their team doctor suspended.

Yet Carmona's subsequent actions made Daum look like Albert Einstein. While under his ban, Carmona flunked another test in January 2006 that meant a lifetime suspension. Carmona fought the ruling, claiming that his B sample had been lost. However, when the lab at the University of California-Los Angeles produced the sample, Carmona tried to prevent its testing. The World Anti-Doping Agency was not amused, and issued a lifetime suspension. Incredibly, Carmona ignored the order, claiming that a Mexican magistrate had issued an injunction allowing him to play, which he did for club side Cruz Azul deep into the 2007 Mexican league playoffs. Threatened with serious sanctions by FIFA, the Mexican federation upheld the ban and threw Cruz Azul out of the competition for playing Carmona.

10. BERNARD LAMA

In the grand scheme of things, Lama's positive test for marijuana in 1997 ranks low on the list of all-time transgressions, but the cost for the French goalkeeper proved steep. Lama was the de facto first-choice keeper for the French national team heading into the 1998 World Cup, which France would host. Yet Lama's positive test saw him lose his starting spot to Fabien Barthez, and although Lama was on the roster for the World Cup, it was Barthez who received all the accolades. Not only did France defeat Brazil 3-0 in the final, but Barthez took home the Yashin award as the best keeper in the tournament, leaving Lama to wonder, "What if?"

Bizarre Injuries

Injuries have scuttled many a promising career in the world of soccer, and the competition for places puts a premium on staying healthy and taking care of one's body. For that reason, teams all over world hire the best conditioning specialists, doctors, and physical therapists in an effort to keep their players on the field. Alas, the soccer industry has yet to find a way to save some players from themselves, especially when they're outside the lines.

1. EMERSON

Ignorance may be bliss, but in the case of Emerson, it cost him a World Cup-winner's medal. Named captain of the Brazil team before the 2002 World Cup, Emerson and his teammates were taking part in a light-hearted practice session just before the start of the tournament, with the midfield lynchpin playing in goal. But when Emerson tried to stop a shot from Rivaldo, he landed awkwardly and separated his shoulder, eliminating him from the entire World Cup.

"[Emerson] is not a goalkeeper, so he doesn't know how to fall properly," Rivaldo told the *Guardian*, without a hint of understatement.

2. **SANTIAGO CANIZARES**

The Spanish international goalkeeper forged his reputation in Spain's La Liga with Valencia, and his adept handling and shot-stopping ensured that he was the first-choice keeper heading into the 2002 World Cup. But in a Mr. Bean moment during the team's training camp in the Spanish town of Jerez, Canizares dropped a bottle of aftershave, and a shard of glass severed a tendon in his foot, forcing him out of the tournament.

The injury kept Canizares out of action for two months, and while he reclaimed his starting spot with Valencia, he was unable to do the same at international level, with Real Madrid's Iker Casillas now first choice.

3. **DAVE BEASANT**

Not to be outdone by Canizares, Beasant proved to be equally error-prone away from the field in 1993 when he knocked a jar of salad dressing off the counter, tried to stop it with his foot, only to have the glass break and cut ligaments in his foot. The injury kept him out of the Southampton lineup for two-and-a-half months.

4. **STEVE MORROW**

On a day that should have been the pinnacle of his professional career, Morrow endured a freak injury that made Canizares look lucky by comparison. Morrow and his Arsenal teammates were celebrating their 2-1 victory over Sheffield Wednesday in the 1993 League Cup final, a game in which Morrow had scored the game-winner. When teammate Tony Adams attempted to lift Morrow onto his shoulders, Morrow fell off and broke his arm, causing him to not only miss the medal ceremony, but it also ruled him out of the FA Cup final later that season. It was prior to that match that Morrow was awarded his League Cup-winner's medal, making it the first—and probably last—time that a player received a medal *before* a cup final.

5. JOHN DURNIN

Leave it to Durnin to turn golf into a contact sport. In 1999, the Portsmouth forward was in the middle of playing a round with teammate Alan McLoughlin when he crashed the golf cart they were driving into a ditch. McLoughlin walked away with a cut face, but Durnin dislocated his elbow and missed six weeks.

Durnin, known as "Johnny Lager" to fans, insisted that they weren't drunk, and that the accident happened because the two were admiring the view instead of eyeing the cart path. Less said the better.

6. ALEX STEPNEY

In the '90s the sight of Manchester United goalkeeper Peter Schmeichel screaming at his defenders made Gordon Ramsay look like he was sedated. Yet Schmeichel's forebear in the United goal went one better, when in the middle of berating his defense against Birmingham City, Stepney dislocated his jaw.

7. SVEIN GRONDALEN

The Norwegian defender was preparing for an international match in the '70s when he injured himself jogging. No, Grondalen did not step in a pothole or get hit by a car. He collided with a moose, with the result that he was forced to pull out of the upcoming match. In the grand scheme of things, Grondalen might have preferred getting hit by a car.

8. JULIO ARCA

Fresh from a Sunderland training session on an English beach in August 2004, Arca thought a refreshing dip in the North Sea would be the perfect pick-me-up. What the Argentine didn't count on was finding a jellyfish in the water that proceeded to sting him in the chest. An allergic reaction ensued with Arca being sent to the hospital. Arca missed a few days training but recovered in time to suit up for Sunderland in the next match against Wigan.

9. MARTIN PALERMO

The Argentine striker had just scored a goal in extra time for Spanish side Villareal in a 2001 Copa del Rey match against Levante. Excited as he was at his extra-time strike, he immediately began celebrating with Villareal's fans by standing on a concrete retaining wall, which collapsed causing Palermo to break his leg. The injury kept him out for six months and caused him to miss the 2002 World Cup.

10. RICHARD WRIGHT

Currently at West Ham, the goalkeeper has shown a unique penchant for self-inflicted injuries. While at Everton, his preseason preparations for the 2003 season were wrecked when he injured his shoulder after falling from a loft. But Wright outdid himself prior to a February 8, 2006, match against Chelsea, when he sprained his ankle while warming up in goal. His foot had landed on a sign instructing players to warm up elsewhere.

Penalty Kick Trivia

The Germans excel at it. The English have been tormented by it. But love it or hate it, the penalty kick, also known as the "kick of death," has been a part of the game for over 100 years, and it has been at the center of some of soccer's most dramatic moments.

1. WILLIAM MCCRUM

A sportsman and businessman from Milford, County Armagh, Northern Ireland, McCrum is widely credited with the invention of the penalty kick in 1890. Appalled at the mayhem occurring in front of goal, McCrum felt that a sanction steeper than a simple indirect free kick was warranted for fouls that denied goal-scoring opportunities. But when McCrum's idea was presented to the International Football Association Board, it was met with derision, the thought being that no Victorian gentleman would ever be so unsporting as to intentionally foul an opponent. Reality prevailed a year later, and the rule was finally approved. Resistance remained, however, as some players, most notably those of English amateur side Corinthians, still felt the sanction was ungentlemanly. As a result, some players just rolled the ball straight to the keeper instead of attempting to score.

2. J. DALTON

An Irishman may have invented the rule, but it was an American playing for a Canadian team who is credited as the first to convert a penalty kick. Less surprising is that according to some eyewitnesses, the kick was incorrectly given.

The match featured a team simply referred to as the Canadians playing Belfast side Linfield on August 29, 1891. A Belfast defender named Gordon was adjudged to have handled the ball in the penalty area, although a match report from the *Belfast Telegraph* alleged that the infraction was "unintentional," thus spawning the lament of defenders everywhere. It was left to an American player known only as J. Dalton to dispatch the spot kick, which earned him a place in the history books.

3. MARTIN PALERMO

If the old Corinthians had a favorite modern-day player, Palermo would have been their man. During Argentina's match against Colombia in the 1999 Copa America, Palermo contrived to miss three penalties in a single match. Palermo struck the crossbar with his first attempt after just five minutes, skied his second attempt over the bar with fifteen minutes to play, and with his team down 3-0 late in the match, offered to take the third. Palermo finally managed to hit the target, but saw his effort saved by Colombian keeper Miguel Calero. "There's always a first time for everything and today I saw it," said Colombian coach Javier Alvarez.

4. ALEX

If Palermo needed lessons on penalty taking, he could do a lot worse than study Brazilian striker Alex. While playing for Cruzeiro in 2003, Alex scored four times from the penalty spot in a Brazilian Championship match against Bahia, with all of the goals coming in the first thirty-seven minutes.

5. **KARL WALD AND MICHAEL ALMOG**

Like calculus and the internal combustion engine, there are numerous claims for the invention of the penalty kick shootout. And while the shootout's contributions to society are debatable, considering that tied games had previously been decided by drawing lots and coin flips, it represented a massive improvement as tiebreakers went.

No doubt inspired, or perhaps disgusted, at seeing a coin flip eliminate Israel in the semifinals of the 1968 Summer Olympics, Israeli Executive Committee member Michael Almog put forward the idea in the August 1969 edition of *Fifa News*. Another proponent of the rule was Wald, a German referee who submitted his proposal to the Bavarian Football Association in 1970. The proposal subsequently moved up soccer's hierarchy and was approved by UEFA and FIFA shortly thereafter, much to the dismay of Englishmen everywhere.

6. **THE WATNEY CUP**

The first time the tiebreaker was used in a professional setting was on August 5, 1970, in the semifinal of a now-defunct preseason tournament called the Watney Cup. The match was contested by Manchester United and Hull City and, after extra time ended 1-1, history was made. United's George Best scored the first penalty shootout goal, but teammate Dennis Law later had his shot saved by Hull goalkeeper Ian McKechnie. McKechnie's joy proved short-lived, however, as he was chosen to take Hull's fifth attempt, and needing to score to keep Hull in the match, he smacked his shot off the bar and over the goal.

7. **THE SHOOTOUT THAT WASN'T**

Scottish side Rangers took the term "cheating the hangman" to extremes in 1972 when they faced off in the second round of the European Cup Winners' Cup against Portuguese side Sporting Lisbon. Rangers won the first leg at home 3-2, and Sporting won the return encounter by the same score, forcing extra time. In the extra session, Rangers' Willie Henderson put the Scots ahead, only for Sporting to equalize with just six minutes remaining. When extra time ended, referee Laurens van Raavens ordered penalties, and when Rangers could convert just one attempt, Sporting prevailed, with goalkeeper Damas being carried off the field by delirious Sporting fans.

There was only one problem. Rangers, by virtue of the "away goals" rule should have won the cup-tie outright, having scored one more goal on the road than Sporting. Rangers' manager Willie Waddell duly tracked down a senior UEFA official, and pointed to the rulebook, claiming that Rangers should be declared the victors. Waddell was judged to be correct, the decision was overturned, and Rangers were declared the winners. As it turns out, Rangers made the most of their reprieve as they later won the entire tournament with a 3-2 win over Dynamo Moscow. Mercifully, penalties weren't needed.

8. **ANTONIN PANENKA**

The first senior level competition to be decided via penalties was the 1976 European Championship final between West Germany and Czechoslovakia, but the shootout went down in history for more reasons than one. The first seven kicks were converted, giving Czechoslovakia a 4-3 lead. But West Germany's Uli Hoeness skied his shot over the bar, setting the stage for Panenka. The entire world, including German keeper Sepp Maier, expected Panenka to blast it to one side. But to the shock and delight of many of those present, Panenka opted to softly chip the ball straight down the middle, and with Maier committing himself with a powerful dive to his left, the ball settled softly into the back of the net. To this day, the move is known as "the Panenka," and Pelé himself stated, "anyone who takes a penalty like that is either a genius or a madman." The result is also the only time in five tries that Germany has failed to win a penalty shootout.

9. 2005 NAMIBIAN CUP

Penalty shootouts are designed to bring a quick end to a long match, but in the case of the first round match between KK Palace and Civics, they might as well have kept on playing. The tiebreaker lasted an incredible twenty-four rounds, forty-eight kicks in all, with KK Palace finally prevailing 17-16. It remains the longest penalty kick shootout in the history of professional soccer.

10. 1994 WORLD CUP

The final of the 1994 edition was a first in many ways. It was the first final to finish 0-0 at the end of regulation. Brazil became the first country to win the cup four times. But it was also the first time a World Championship had ever been decided on penalties, and it was Brazil who would prevail, as Italian legends Roberto Baggio and Franco Baresi both missed their attempts. It wouldn't be the last a time a World Cup would be decided on penalties either. The 1999 women's event saw the United States triumph over China via spot kicks, and the same method was used on the men's side in 2006 when Italy prevailed over France.

Animal House

Whether it's invasions on the field, in the locker room, or the boardroom, the animal kingdom has never been far from the action in the world of soccer. The 1923 FA Cup final was called "The White Horse Final" after a standing-room-only crowd was kept at bay by a policeman's horse. Then there was the English dog, Pickles, who helped recover the stolen Jules Rimet Trophy in 1966. But those proved to be far from the only two animal-infused incidents to grace the world's favorite sport.

1. THE DUCK HUNT

The life of a goalkeeper is kind of like a movie starring Dwayne "The Rock" Johnson—short bursts of action followed by long spells of boredom. No one knew this better than Bayern Munich goalkeeper Sepp Maier, who played during one of Bayern's more dominant spells in the '70s. But on May 15, 1976, in a match between Bayern and Vfl Bochum, Maier was presented with a golden opportunity to alleviate the monotony. With Bayern camped out in the opposition half, a duck landed in Maier's penalty area, and to pass the time Maier did his best to bring something exotic to the family dinner table. As it turns out, Maier was a better goalkeeper than he was a hunter. He resorted to several full-scale dives, but the duck managed to evade his clutches every time, much to the delight of the crowd.

2. CHIC BRODIE
Brodie's memories of his own encounter with an on-field interloper are significantly less fond. During a 1970 match between Brentford and Colchester, a dog invaded the field and went for the ball just as Brodie, the Brentford goalkeeper, was collecting a back-pass. Brodie collided with the dog, fell awkwardly, and ended up shattering his kneecap—an injury that ended his career.

3. SACRIFICIAL LAMBS
When Bulgarian second division side PFC Etar Veliko Tarnovo began the 2006 season winless after seven games, it was decided that drastic measures were needed. So a priest was hired to sacrifice a lamb and smear the blood on the goalposts. Initially, the maneuver did not put the club in good stead with the Lord, as the team lost their next match to PFC Beli Orli by a score of 2-1. But Etar did shake off their poor form sufficiently to avoid relegation that season.

4. NOT SO SILENT LAMBS
Unlike their Bulgarian counterparts, a better fate awaited some sheep in Croatia, especially those belonging to Ivica Supe, a player with third division side Zagora FC. It turns out the club's sole sponsor is a shepherd who agreed to give the team's leading scorer a sheep for every goal scored. So with Supe sitting on sixteen goals, the sponsor decided it was time to pay up.

"It was a surprise, I just don't know where I will keep them," Supe said about his new herd.

"We are only a small club, and we could not get anyone else to sponsor us," the Ananova news service quoted a club spokesman as saying. "There is no industry in the area, it's only a small village, and we were delighted when Mr. [Josko] Bralic offered to support us with sheep."

5. BIRD'S-EYE VIEW

Matches are delayed for all kinds of reasons, with injury the usual culprit. But a Euro 2008 qualifier between Finland and Belgium was delayed six minutes when an owl invaded the pitch, forcing several players to duck out of its way. After taking up temporary residence atop each of the goals, the owl, nicknamed Bubi by the Finnish press, watched from a railing behind one of the goals. Finland won the match 2-0, with the owl being adopted as a mascot. Unfortunately, the owl went missing during the rest of qualification, which might explain Finland enduring four 0-0 draws during the remainder of their campaign. The wayward owl was later named Resident of the Year by a Finnish journalists' association.

6. PIG IN A POKEY

Six minutes may have proved a mild diversion, but a 2003 Austrian Cup match between SPG Wattens/Wacker and SV Salzburg was delayed for twenty minutes when a piglet, believed to have been smuggled in by a fan, made its way onto the field. The little swine proceeded to give six match stewards the run around before finally being corralled, all while fans cheered the piglet's exploits. It was later taken to an animal shelter.

7. SAVED BY THE . . . FROGS?

In 1977, the New York Cosmos traveled to the balmy climes

of Bermuda for preseason training. One of their matches involved playing the Bermuda U-21 national team, and as befits such a mismatch the Cosmos had their way with their hosts, taking a 6-0 lead into halftime. The lead was extended to 11-0 when the soccer gods decided that enough was enough, unleashing a plague on the participants. As general manager Clive Toye recounts in *A Kick in the Grass*, "scores of frogs; huge massive frogs emerged from the turf." The game was subsequently abandoned.

8. A BIRD IN THE HAND . . .

It was a moment that would have made Monty Python's Flying Circus proud. John Lambie, during one of his three stints as manager of Scottish side Partick Thistle, had been getting a bit of smack-talk thrown his way by player Declan Roche. Lambie responded by reaching into a box of dead pigeons and according to the *BBC,* "slapped him around the face with one." So just how did Lambie come to have a box of decomposing pigeons in his office? It turns out that the Scottish coach was a breeder of pigeons and was in the process of burying some of his deceased brood. The folks at the People for the Ethical Treatment of Animals were likely not impressed.

9. TAKING ONE FOR THE TEAM

On the last day of the 1987 season, Torquay United were facing relegation from the football league, needing to at least draw their game against Crewe Alexandra to avoid the drop. With seven minutes to go, and Torquay losing 2-1, a police dog bit midfielder Jim McNichol. It took four minutes to treat McNichol's injury, and as luck would have it, Torquay's Paul Dobson equalized in the third minute of stoppage time, thus preserving the club's league status.

10. GETTING SQUIRRELLY

The scene was the first leg of the 2006 UEFA Champions League semifinal between Arsenal and Villareal. The venue was Arsenal's soon-to-be-torn-down home, Highbury. And with the Champions League anthem still ringing in everyone's ears, a squirrel decided to partake in the festivities by invading the field just ten minutes into the match. With the crowd chanting, "squirrel, squirrel," the furry interloper made a few dashes across Arsenal goalkeeper Jens Lehmann's penalty area before disappearing into the stands. "He was too quick for me," Lehmann later recounted. Arsenal's 1-0 win made the night even more memorable.

Lies, Damn Lies, and Urban Legends

In this age of *Punk'd*, it's best for soccer's biggest names to look at any potential career opportunity with a hefty amount of skepticism. But that hasn't stopped some notables from being caught in the midst of some eye-popping scams. And on some occasions, it was a player doing the scamming.

1. SVEN-GORAN ERIKSSON

Just five months before Eriksson would coach England at the 2006 World Cup, a man claiming to be a rich Arab businessman approached him. The two discussed the possibility of Eriksson leaving the England post for a job with English Premier League side Aston Villa. It turns out the Arab "sheikh" was none other than *News of the World* undercover reporter Mazher Mahmood, and the fact that Eriksson was already planning his departure led some to question his commitment to the England cause. But even more damaging were his discussions of various players, including his assertion that Rio Ferdinand was "lazy sometimes" and Michael Owen "unhappy" at club side Newcastle United. The disclosures forced Eriksson to engage in some major damage control once the scam was revealed. As it turned out, England fell at the quarterfinal stage and Eriksson was soon on his way to Manchester City.

2. JOSE ANTONIO REYES

In 2005, repeated rumors surfaced stating that the Arsenal attacker was homesick and wanted to return to his native Spain. Reyes denied the rumors, but the truth was revealed during a crank call with Spanish radio personality Cadena Cope who claimed to be Real Madrid Sporting Director Emilio Butragueno. With Cope indicating that Real were interested in acquiring Reyes, the Arsenal player not only admitted his interest but called some of his Arsenal teammates "bad people." The talk proved prophetic as Reyes was loaned to Real Madrid for the 2006–07 season before securing a permanent move to city rivals Atletico Madrid.

3. EDDIE FORREST

In this instance, it was a case of crime paying off for everyone, and it wasn't the media but a fellow professional who perpetrated the scam. Forrest had signed a part-time contract with Scottish outfit Arbroath, when a caller claiming to be Raith Rovers chairman Danny Smith offered Forrest a full-time deal. Forrest, with Arbroath's blessing jumped at the move, with Arbroath moving to sign Paul Browne in his stead. But when Forrest contacted Smith to finalize the deal, he realized he had been tricked. The caller was none other than Browne, leaving Forrest without a club. Once the sting was discovered, Arbroath sacked Browne and agreed to take Forrest back, but Forrest eventually signed a contract with Scottish Premier League side Partick Thistle. That left Browne, who claimed the prank went much farther than he ever intended, to end up on the books of Arbroath.

4. BRISTOL ROVERS

During the 1998–99 season, Bristol Rovers were playing in the third tier of English soccer and, desperate to improve their home results, employed two "experts" in the practice of Feng Shui, which is the art of arranging objects to achieve balance and harmony in one's environment. The alleged specialists, Guy de Beaujeu and Patrick Stockhausen, proceeded to implement a number of changes. These included placing an ornamental ceramic frog above the entrance to Memorial Stadium, putting a fish tank behind one of the goals, and placing plants in the four corners of the home locker room and wind chimes in various locations around the stadium. Suffice it say, the changes had no effect. Bristol Rovers proceeded to go 2-3-2 at home during the rest of the season. Even worse, de Beaujeu and Stockhausen later admitted that the entire stunt had been concocted as a means of promoting their comedy series.

5. KARL POWER

The pre-match photo of the starting eleven is one of those barely noticed soccer rituals. But the team photo of Manchester United before they took the field against Bayern Munich in the 2001 UEFA Champions League made headlines when it was discovered that an imposter, in full Manchester United uniform, had somehow wormed his way into the pre-game portrait. The photographic gatecrasher wasn't noticed until after the match, at which time a full-scale manhunt ensued. Power soon confessed to his stealthy pitch invasion, claiming that the stunt was two years in the making and that he had conned his way into the ground by pretending to be part of a TV crew. United defender Gary Neville nearly spoiled the stunt when he pointed Power out, but the life-long fan held his ground and made an interesting bit of history. "It must be the biggest and best football sting of all time," crowed Power.

6. RYAN GIGGS

Power's stunt wouldn't be the last to be perpetrated on a Manchester United player. Just two years later, fan Jamie Mardon grabbed a microphone from the Millenium Stadium press area and proceeded to conduct an on-field interview with Ryan Giggs. The United winger answered one question before realizing that the joke was on. Mardon was soon arrested for "field invasion."

7. KNUT TORBJØRN EGGEN

Coaches are always on the lookout for new players, but Eggen's desire got the better of him in 2006. Eggen had received what was purported to be an email from former Norwegian goalkeeper Emile Baron in which he recommended a South African player by the name of Given Mabasa. But a quick trial soon revealed the truth. "After what I have seen in training, I guarantee that he has never played high level football," said Eggen. "So I just have to admit that I have been completely fooled."

8. GRAEME SOUNESS

Perhaps Eggen was being a bit hard on himself, especially when compared to what happened to Souness while managing Southampton. In 1996, Souness received a phone call allegedly from Liberian international George Weah, claiming that a player named Ali Dia was his cousin, a Senegalese international, and had played for French side Paris St. Germain. It turns out the caller was Dia's agent and that Dia's playing résumé was a complete fabrication; but that didn't stop Souness from signing Dia to a one-month contract. The truth was discovered when Dia took the field at the thirty-two-minute mark in a league match against Leeds United. His play was so spectacularly poor that he was substituted for after just fifty-three minutes on the field and was released shortly thereafter. Dia is widely regarded as the worst player ever to see minutes in the EPL.

9. STEPHEN IRELAND

The dead grandmother has been an excuse used to avoid homework assignments and second dates the world over, so Ireland thought he'd use it not once, but twice. The Manchester City midfielder had just finished playing for the Irish national team in a Euro 2008 qualifier against Slovakia when his girlfriend rang to tell him that his grandmother had died. The Football Association of Ireland, in a humanitarian gesture, hired Ireland a private jet to fly him home to attend the funeral. But when said grandmother revealed that she was still very much alive, Ireland claimed it had all been a mistake and that it was his *other* grandmother who had died. But when that granny proved to be still breathing as well, Ireland was forced to confess that the real reason for his fibbing was that his girlfriend had suffered a miscarriage, and that they both figured a return trip home would be more acceptable if the excuse was a dead grandmother. Leave it to Ireland's club manager Sven-Goran Eriksson to put it best when he told the online version of the *Sunday Times*, "Whatever problem you have in life, when you talk to your club or country and the managers, keep to the truth. Do not lie. That is stupid."

10. YARDIS ALPOLFO

In April 2003, Scottish side Rangers FC made the stunning announcement on their website that they had just acquired

Yardis Alpolfo from Turkish club Galatasaray for a whopping $15 million transfer fee. Reuters and Teletext duly passed on the news . . . without realizing that the date of the press release was April 1 and that "Yardis Alpolfo" is an anagram for April Fools' Day. Rangers quickly informed the two agencies that the news was in fact a hoax.

Match Fixing and Betting Scandals

For all the joys that soccer has created around the globe, the game's seamier side has reared its head on numerous occasions, with cases of match-fixing blighting soccer at various points throughout its history.

1. ENGLAND (1900)

One of the first recorded match-fixing scandals occurred when Burnley goalkeeper Jack Hillman attempted to bribe players of Nottingham Forest. Burnley needed to win the match in order to avoid relegation to a lower division, and Hillman offered the Forest players £2 each to "go easy." When Burnley found themselves down 2-0 at halftime, Hillman upped the ante to £5 a head. It didn't work as Forest prevailed 4-0. When the English FA got wind of the plot, they suspended Hillman for one year, despite his protestations of innocence.

2. ENGLAND (1964)

How much does it cost an international player to ruin his soccer career? In the case of Sheffield Wednesday center back Peter Swan just £50, which is the amount he bet on his side to lose a league match against Ipswich Town in 1964.

The bet was made at the behest of a former player named Jimmy Gauld, who even during his playing days had a second career fixing games. In this instance, Gauld convinced Swan and two of his teammates, Tony Kay and David Layne, to place their bets on the aforementioned match and recorded their conversations in the process. Wednesday lost 2-0.

In an act of immense stupidity, Gauld sold the entire story to the *Sunday People* for £7,000, and with the help of Gauld's tape recordings, he and a total of nine players were convicted of defrauding bookmakers. Gauld received the maximum sentence of four years in prison and a £5,000 fine, while the others served less than four months. As for their playing careers, all were given lifetime bans that were lifted after seven years.

3. **BRAZIL (2005)**

These days, with players now earning comfortable livings, the target of most gamblers is no longer the performers on the field but the referees who adjudicate their matches. That was precisely what happened to referees Edilson Pereira de Carvalho and Paulo Jose Danelon who influenced the outcome of matches on behalf of an international betting syndicate. Carvalho was over $30,000 in debt, and he proceeded to charge between $4,000 and $6,000 per match in effort to wipe out his balance.

Brazilian police, who recorded Carvalho speaking with members of the syndicate to throw matches in the Brazilian Championship, uncovered the plot, and the investigation then spread to Danelon, a second-division referee. The duo was later banned for life.

The scandal threw the results of the 2005 Brazilian Championship into chaos. The matches refereed by Carvalho were annulled allowing Corinthians to leapfrog Internacional in the standings and claim the championship.

4. GERMANY (2005)

Nothing says, "We're ready to host the World Cup," quite like a match-fixing scandal, but that was what host nation Germany faced in the fall of 2005 when referee Robert Hoyzer was caught throwing matches on behalf of a Croatian betting ring. Hoyzer's downfall was that he was a tad too enthusiastic in carrying out his duties. Specifically, a German Cup match between third division Paderborn and Bundesliga side Hamburg ended in a shocking 4-2 decision for the underdogs. In that match, Hoyzer called two dubious penalties in Paderborn's favor and sent off Hamburg striker Emile Mpenza for dissent.

The conspiracy was later found to include another referee, Dominic Marks, as well as former Bundesliga player Steffen Karl who by then was playing in the German third division. Still, German soccer officials were relieved that the scandal had not spread to the Bundesliga, and by the time the World Cup took place in 2006 the news was largely forgotten.

5. ITALY (2006)

Perhaps the biggest match-fixing case to rock soccer in recent years was the Calciopoli scandal that plagued the highest levels of Italian soccer. The conspiracy involved the executives of several clubs—including those of Juventus, A.C. Milan, Fiorentina, Lazio, and Reggina—who conspired with Italian soccer officials to influence which referees would get assigned to their games. At the center of the scandal was Juventus general manager Luciano Moggi, who with the help of wiretaps was found to have had numerous conversations with Italian soccer officials over who would referee Juve's matches.

The penalties involved were severe. Juventus were stripped of their 2005 and 2006 league titles, demoted to the second division, and had nine points deducted. The rest were allowed to remain in Serie A with point deductions, but it could have been much worse. The original point penalties had been drastically reduced on appeal, and A.C. Milan, who was initially tossed out of the 2006–07 UEFA Champions League, was allowed back in and eventually won the competition.

6. ITALY (1980)

This particular journey into soccer hell was different in that it was the gamblers who got burned, and while some players also went down in flames, for more than a few there was a happy ending.

This particular scandal began with two Roman businessmen, Massimo Cruciano and Alvaro Trinca, convincing players from several clubs to throw matches. Or so they thought. Many of the match-fixing attempts backfired, plunging the duo into debt, and with bookmakers breathing down their neck they too went public. The result was that Lazio and A.C. Milan were relegated to Serie B while more than thirty players were arrested. Incredibly, there were no laws on the books for sporting fraud, so no players were convicted, but all were given playing suspensions of up to three years.

The most famous player involved was Italian international Paolo Rossi who was given a three-year ban. The suspension was later reduced to two years, which allowed him to return just in time for the 1982 World Cup. The media howled over such favorable treatment, but after Rossi led the Azzurri to the title, scoring six goals in the process, the din subsided. Such was the goodwill following that tournament that the rest of the players had their suspensions lifted.

7. FRANCE (1993)

The spring of 1993 was the best of times for French club Olympique Marseille. The team had just won their fifth consecutive league title and also became the first French side to win the UEFA Champions League. But the good times lasted even shorter than usual after it was revealed that OM owner Bernard Tapie had orchestrated a bribe to players of French side Valenciennes to throw their match against OM. The match took place the weekend before the Champions League final, and Tapie wanted to not only make sure none of his players were injured but also that his team would secure the league championship. Valenciennes duly complied and lost the match 1-0, and OM were league champions again.

The whistle was blown by one of the bribed Valenciennes players, Jacques Glassman, and police subsequently found 250,000 francs buried in the garden of teammate Christophe Robert's mother-in-law. Robert and teammates Jean-Jacques Eydelie and Jorge Burruchaga were given lengthy bans. OM was stripped of their league title, but not their Champions League crown, and both teams were relegated to the second division. Tapie, who claimed that the investigation was aimed at ruining his budding political career, was sentenced to two years in prison for his role in the scam.

8. ENGLAND (1999)

So what does a match-fixer do when players, coaches, or referees aren't available to influence the outcome? They do what an Asian betting syndicate did in 1999, when they tried to sabotage the floodlights at Charlton Athletic's home stadium, The Valley. The idea is to bet on games involving a heavy favorite, wait until the second half when an abandoned match will still pay out to bettors, and if the score is favorable, literally turn off the lights, in this case via remote control.

The tactic worked in two English Premier League matches in 1997, one between West Ham United and Crystal Palace, and another between Wimbledon and Arsenal. But a Charlton security guard who was in on the 1999 scheme tried to bring in an accomplice, a co-worker who immediately informed the authorities. The guard and three others were later jailed for conspiracy to cause a public nuisance.

9. SOUTH AFRICA (2004)

The police called it "Operation Dribble." The South African soccer authorities called it the worst scandal to ever hit Africa's most profitable league. And in the end, it amounted to some eye-catching headlines but little more. In this case, thirty-three referees, match commissioners, and team officials were snared in a probe that began at the behest of South African Soccer Association head Molefi Oliphant. Yet only four people were ever convicted, with many of the court cases thrown out for lack of sufficient evidence.

10. VIETNAM (2005)

Match fixing usually takes place at the club level, but in this case the skullduggery occurred at the 2005 Southeast Asian Games. Eight Vietnamese players pledged to beat Myanmar by a score of just 1-0 and were paid around $30,000 for their "efforts." The ringleaders, midfielder Le

Quoc Vuong and club player Truong Tan Hai who acted as the go-between, went to jail for their role in the affair, while the other six were given suspended sentences.

Fair Play

In an age when sportsmanship almost always takes a back seat to more competitive urges, there have been those moments when more altruistic impulses have carried the day.

1. ARSENAL

One of the long-held traditions of soccer is that a team will intentionally kick the ball out of bounds so that an injured player, be it either teammate or opponent, can be attended to. But such protocol escaped Arsenal forward Nwankwo Kanu during a 1999 FA Cup match between the Gunners and Sheffield United. United had played the ball out of bounds so one their players could receive treatment. But instead of allowing his opponent to retain possession, Kanu, making his Arsenal debut, streaked toward goal and passed for Marc Overmars to score what would prove to be the game-winning goal in a 2-1 victory. The Sheffield United players were incensed, but Arsenal manager Arsene Wegner came upon a novel idea. "I offered the replay because it wasn't right to win that way—it wasn't Arsenal," Wenger said. "The best we can do is offer to replay the game here against Sheffield United."

The offer was accepted, and the rematch took place

eight days later with Arsenal once again prevailing 2-1, this time without controversy.

2. MORTEN WIEGHORST
Denmark was playing Iran in the 2003 Carlsberg Cup, when an Iranian player, thinking he had heard the halftime whistle, picked up the ball in his own penalty area. What he had heard instead was a whistle from the crowd, and the referee awarded Denmark a penalty kick. But after consulting with head coach Morten Olsen, Wieghorst missed the penalty on purpose. "It was unfair to try and capitalize on that," said Wieghorst. "The Iranian player had no idea what had happened." Denmark lost the match 1-0, but Wieghorst was given an award by the International Fairplay Committee.

3. GARY LINEKER
Lineker enjoyed one of the finest careers of any English striker. His forty-eight international goals are the second-most for an English player, and he continued those exploits at club level, scoring over 200 times. But as remarkable as those numbers are, perhaps the most stunning number surrounding Lineker's career was zero, which is the combined number of yellow and red cards he received in his fifteen-year career, a stunning mark given the physical nature of English soccer. Such was Lineker's approach to the game that he won FIFA's Fair Play award in 1990.

4. LEICESTER CITY AND NOTTINGHAM FOREST
The two English sides squared off in the 2007 English League Cup, and Forest were winning 1-0 at halftime when Leicester defender Clive Clark suffered a heart attack, forcing the game's abandonment. Rules stipulated that the game had to be restarted from scratch, but in a sporting gesture

Leicester allowed Forest to score straight from the kick-off—with goalkeeper Paul Smith doing the honors—so that the original scoreline could be restored. The plan was the brainchild of Leicester owner Milan Mandaric, manager Gary Megson, and managing director Tim Davies. "It was a gift from everyone at Leicester City for the way Forest behaved in the first game," Mandaric said. "We wanted to show that morality and fair play are not dead in the game." Leicester's charity didn't end up costing them either. They won the match 3-2.

5. PAOLO DI CANIO
Di Canio had a well-earned reputation as one of the game's most volatile characters during his seventeen-year playing career, and he was once suspended in 1998 for pushing over a referee after receiving a red card. But the Italian made the front pages for all the right reasons in 2000 while playing for West Ham United. In a league match against Everton, opposition goalkeeper Paul Gerrard was lying on the ground after he had twisted his knee while making a clearance. When a subsequent cross came into the box, Di Canio was perfectly positioned to take advantage, but instead of heading the ball in, he caught it instead so that play would be stopped and the injured Gerrard could be attended to. This display of sportsmanship won Di Canio FIFA's Fair Play Award in 2001.

6. OMAR LORENZO DEVANNI
They're called derby matches, games between local rivals where the pressure and tension are worn like an anvil and gamesmanship is compulsory. But in 1967, Devanni rose above such burdens during a Colombian league match between bitter adversaries Sante Fe and Millonarios. With the

score tied 2-2 late in the match, Devanni, a forward for Sante Fe, tripped over his own feet, only to be awarded a penalty by the referee. But instead of accepting the charity, Devanni purposely shot the ball wide instead.

7. MICHAEL GALEA AND STEPHEN AZZOPARDI

During a 2004 Maltese league match between Birkirkara and St. Patrick, Birkirkara were leading 2-0 and poised to score again through Galea when St. Patrick defender Arnold Buttigieg went down injured. Acting on instructions from Birkirkara manager Azzopardi, Galea pulled up and stopped play rather than press what was deemed to be an unfair advantage.

8. OZGURCAN OZCAN

It was in 2005 when Ozcan did what the English wish Diego Maradona had done in the 1986 World Cup. In the more recent incident during a Turkish youth league match between Galatasaray and Denizlispor, Ozcan scored an apparent goal with his head, but immediately afterward the Galatasaray forward admitted he had used his hand. The goal was nullified and Ozcan was shown a yellow card, but he later earned an award from the International Fairplay Committee.

9. MICHAEL PARKHURST

Defenders are usually known for their willingness to use any means necessary to stop an opponent, and that includes a heavy reliance on tactical fouls. But Parkhurst, a defender with the New England Revolution of Major League Soccer, has shown that fouls need not be a part of a defender's repertoire. During his rookie year of 2005, Parkhurst committed a scant six fouls during the entire *season*, a mark he bettered in 2007 when he was adjudged to have had only five infractions. Such discipline earned him the MLS Fair Play Award in 2007.

10. FRANK ORDENEWITZ

The scene was a 1987 Bundesliga match between Werder Bremen and Cologne, when Ordenewitz handled a Cologne shot in his own penalty area. The foul went unnoticed by the referee, but when the Cologne players protested, the referee confronted Ordenewitz who admitted to the infraction. Cologne was awarded a penalty kick as a result, and went on to win the match 2-0. Not all of Ordenewitz's Bremen teammates were impressed, but FIFA decided to make note of the show of sportsmanship, awarding Ordenewitz its Fair Play award the following year.

The Rogues Gallery

Every successful team has its resident hatchet man, but when going up against some of them, opponents were always careful to pack their titanium shin guards.

1. ANDONI GOIKOETXEA

If there was ever a reason for a forward to have his orthopedic surgeon on speed dial, Goikoetxea was it. The "Butcher of Bilbao" was a fearsome tackler who once broke the ankle of Diego Maradona with a horrendous challenge from behind. Adding bad taste to injury, Goikoetxea commemorated the deed by placing the offending shoe in a glass display case.

2. JOSE BATISTA

The Uruguayan defender was a feared opponent in the best of times, but Batista outdid himself in the 1986 World Cup when he was sent off for taking out Scotland forward Gordon Strachan after a scant fifty-six seconds. The real miracle wasn't so much the speed of the red card—which set a World Cup record that still stands—but the fact that Strachan lived to tell the tale of Batista's thuggery.

3. NOBBY STILES

Norbert is a moniker one normally doesn't associate with one of the game's most intimidating midfielders, but "Nobby" provided the steel for the England side that prevailed in the 1966 World Cup, and his gap-toothed visage would have earned him a guest spot in the movie *Halloween*. Stiles is credited with spawning the holding midfielder role so prevalent in today's game. Of particular note was Stiles' marking job in the semifinals on Portugal's creative dynamo, Eusebio. Many bemoaned Stiles' lack of flair but an equal number admitted his importance to England's success.

4. CLAUDIO GENTILE

Gentile is perhaps the most inappropriately named defender of all time, as there was nothing gentle about this Italian mainstay. This was especially true during Italy's run to the 1982 World Cup, where Gentile kicked lumps out of Diego Maradona in Italy's first second-phase match, and then repeated the feat against Brazil's Zico in the next game. England's Kevin Keegan later remarked that Gentile was the kind of player who preferred to swap shirts with an opponent during the game instead of after.

5. LEONEL SANCHEZ

The Chilean stands out in one of the most brutal chapters in World Cup history, the infamous "Battle of Santiago" between Chile and Italy at the 1962 World Cup. After two Italian journalists had made disparaging remarks about Chile prior to the match, the two teams engaged in a free-for-all, with referee Ken Aston siding with the hosts more often than not. Italy's Giorgio Ferrini had already been sent off when Sanchez responded to a steady stream of kicks from

Mario David by flattening him with a left hook. David responded by kicking Sanchez in the neck. Incredibly, Davis was sent off while Sanchez not only stayed on the field, but is reported to have later broken the nose of Umberto Maschio. Sanchez was later given a "letter of admonishment" from FIFA but ended up tying for top scoring honors in the tournament with five other players.

6. BENJAMIN MASSING
The opening match of the 1990 World Cup bore a closer resemblance to an episode of *Kung Fu* than it did to a soccer match. There had already been one expulsion when Argentina's Claudio Caniggia had a run up field ended by Massing's flying tackle, one in which the Cameroon defender lost his shoe in the process. Massing was already on a yellow card, but his assault earned a straight red, forcing Cameroon to finish the match with nine men. The Indomitable Lions still won the match 1-0.

7. GRAEME SOUNESS
Souness narrowly edges out Gentile for the most intimidating moustache of all time, but there was more to the Scot's game than mere looks. In his debut for Rangers against Hibernian, Souness was sent off after a just thirty-four minutes for two yellow cards, the second of which he earned for a challenge on George McCluskey when he cheekily claimed, "my boot ran up his leg." The challenge sparked a twenty-one-man melee with the Hibs keeper the only spectator.

8. VINNIE JONES
The self-styled tough guy of English soccer, Jones once earned a yellow card just five seconds into a match against Manchester City when he upended City midfielder Peter Reid

straight from the kickoff. Jones was later sent off in the match, one of ten red cards he received in his career. That expulsion went along with forty-two cautions he received in his career. Jones was also the presenter of a video called *Soccer's Hard Men* featuring the "greatest hits" of Jones and others. The English Football Association was not amused, and fined Jones £20,000 as a result. Jones later went on to greater fame as an actor in such movies as *Lock, Stock, and Two Smoking Barrels* and *Mean Machine.*

9. ROY KEANE

When the red mist descended on Keane, it was best to hide the women, children, and any stray tibias that happened to be in the area. Case in point was his horrific tackle on Manchester City midfielder Alf Inge Haaland, which severely injured the Norwegian's knee. Keane later admitted in his autobiography that he had intentionally injured Haaland due to a long-simmering feud. The admission drew Keane a hefty fine of £150,000 and a five-match ban from the English FA.

10. PAOLO MONTERO

In a league as notoriously physical as Italy's Serie A, it takes some doing to set the all-time record for red cards, but Montero did just that in nine seasons with Juventus. Ironically, Montero was also regarded as a skillful defender whose passing out of the back was often immaculate, but uncompromising doesn't even begin to describe his style of defending.

Misbehaving Mascots

Mascots are intended to add a bit of frivolity to the trappings of a professional soccer game, although truth be told, they rank just below "sideline reporter" in terms of thankless jobs. But despite their intended entertainment value, there have been a select few who have attracted attention for all the wrong reasons.

1. KINGSLEY ROYAL
The lion-like mascot for English Premier League side Reading F.C. earned the dubious distinction of being given his marching orders by referee Mike Riley during an April 2007 league match with Newcastle United. His offense? Operating so close to the touchline that it made it hard for the linesman to determine if it was Kingsley, who wears a Reading replica shirt, or an actual Reading player who was in an offside position. "I can see where the referee was getting confused," said Reading manager Steve Coppell after the game. "[Kingsley] does look like so many of my players."

2. JUDE THE CAT
Alas, it wasn't the first time such confusion reigned. Back in 2005, the mascot for English second-tier side Queens

Kingsley the Reading mascot is banished from the side of the field by match referee Mike Riley during the Barclays Premiership match between Reading and Newcastle United at the Madejski Stadium on April 30, 2007. Alas, Kingsley is not the only mascot to have run afoul of the authorities.
Ryan Pierse/Getty Images

Park Rangers was sent to the locker room as well. "How can I be mistaken for a player?" Jude lamented to the *BBC*. "I'm a seven-foot black cat! We're waiting to hear from the [English Football Association]. I might be banned from the touchline or have to change my kit. And if that's not bad enough, I've been told my smoked salmon and cream might be taken away."

3. PELLIE THE ELEPHANT
The mascot for Scottish Third Division side Dumbarton F.C. holds the unofficial record for the quickest sending off by a mascot. It took a cozy four minutes for Pellie to be ejected,

when it was discovered his yellow jersey clashed with that of visitors Raith Rovers.

4. ROBBIE THE BOBBIE
Talk about ironic overload. The mascot with one of the longer rap sheets is Bury F.C.'s Robbie, who is decked out as a policeman. He was ejected no fewer than three times in 2001, the second time for a fight with Cardiff City's Barclay the Bluebird. The final straw came following his patented goal celebration, which consisted of a thirty-yard dash, belly-flop, and then mooning opposition spectators. According to the *BBC*, Robbie was finally fired by club management for "stupidity."

5. CHADDY THE OWL
Another repeat offender, Oldham Athletic's mascot Chaddy, also ran afoul of the referee in 2000 when one of the assistant referee's mistook him for a player. But Chaddy really made news in September 2004 for a "brawl" with Bloomfield the Bear of league rivals Blackpool F.C., in which Chaddy ripped the head off his rival. Incredibly, Bloomfield the Bear filed a complaint with police. Said Chaddy to the *Manchester Evening News*, "I couldn't have hurt anyone because I was wearing big foam boots."

6. WOLVERHAMPTON WOLFIE
It was a case of life imitating art—sort of. With Wolverhampton in the process of skunking Bristol City 6-1, Wolfie engaged in a free-for-all with "The Three Little Pigs," the mascots from a local window glazing company. Official Bristol City mascot City Cat then joined in, and turned the tables on Wolfie before match stewards separated all the parties. Wolfie's list of offenses also includes set-tos with

Bolton's Lofty the Lion, and West Bromwich Albion's Baggie the Bird.

7. PAISLEY PANDA

The mascot for Scottish club St. Mirren was fired after wiping his backside with a jersey from opponents Falkirk. The mascot was already on double-secret probation for an incident the season before that the *BBC* described as "gesturing at Queen of the South fans with an inflatable sheep."

8. MANSFIELD VS. HARROWGATE

Another case of a faux fight gone awry. During a December 2007 FA Cup match between the two sides, Mansfield's Sammy the Stag and Harrowgate's seven-foot-tall beaver mascot were engaging in a play fight that evolved into what the *Guardian* called "a bout of mud wrestling."

9. CYRIL THE SWAN

If there were ever a Vinnie Jones Award for mascots, Swansea City's Cyril would win it in a walk. The Swan's reign of terror began in February 2001, when a fight with Millwall's Zampa the Lion ended with Cyril ripping off Zampa's head and drop-kicking it into the stands. Cyril went on to scuffle with a Norwich City director, and was once fined £1,000 for a one-bird pitch invasion following a Swansea goal during an FA Cup match against Millwall.

10. H'ANGUS THE MONKEY

If Hartlepool United's mascot has proven anything, it's that notoriety does pay. The name H'Angus is a pun based on the story that, during the Napoleonic Wars, the residents of Hartlepool allegedly found a monkey in French military regalia that had served aboard a French ship that sank off the coast. They then hanged the monkey on suspicions that it was a French spy. As a result, the residents have been referred to unflatteringly as "monkey hangers." When it came to naming their mascot, the fans of Hartlepool United turned the joke around, and H'Angus was born.

It wasn't long before H'Angus got into trouble. He was ejected by stewards for cavorting with an inflatable doll during a 2006 league match at Blackpool, and another time for rude gestures toward a female steward in 2000. So what did H'Angus do for his next trick? In 2007, the mascot, otherwise known as Stuart Drummond, ran for Mayor of Hartlepool, and won with 52.1 percent of the vote.

Soccer Celebrities

There was a time in the United States when celebrities would sooner reveal membership in the Communist Party than admit an affinity for soccer, but such has been the sport's growth in the last twenty years that espousing a love for "the beautiful game" has almost become trendy. Yet there are some famous faces whose love of soccer goes way beyond just casual interest.

1. JON STEWART
Prior to his rise to comedic stardom, Stewart played for William and Mary College as a winger (one can assume left), scoring ten goals in his collegiate career. The most memorable of these was against Connecticut, which clinched his team a spot in the NCAA tournament.

"It was a typical garbage goal, and like many of the goals I scored, was based on attitude," Stewart told SI.com's Richard Deitsch. "Even Pelé would agree I was not playing the beautiful game. I was playing the annoying game."

2. DREW CAREY
The comedian never played the game but has become a certified soccer junky. Not only has Carey become a fan of

Scottish side Rangers, as well as a Los Angeles Galaxy season ticket holder, but he has now become a part owner of an MLS side that will begin play in Seattle in 2009. Adding to Carey's soccer street-cred is that he's become a legitimate soccer photographer, scoring a press credential to the 2006 World Cup where he followed the U.S. national team, and published photos under the pseudonym Brooks Parkenridge.

3. ANTHONY LAPAGLIA

The *Without a Trace* star actually did play the game in his younger days, playing in Australia's National Soccer League with Adelaide City and West Adelaide. Now that LaPaglia's playing days are behind him, he's moved to the business side of the game as one of the owners of NSL side Sydney FC. LaPaglia is also one of the movers behind the Los Angeles-based amateur side Hollywood F.C.

4. ANDREW SHUE

The former *Melrose Place* star is another celebrity with deep soccer roots. Shue played collegiate soccer at Dartmouth where he was an All-Ivy League selection in 1988. Shue then played professionally in Zimbabwe for Bulawayo Highlanders while teaching math to children, and even latched on with the Los Angeles Galaxy for the 1996 season, tallying the winning assist in a 2-1 win over the San Jose Clash. Shue later went on to help produce the soccer movie *Gracie*.

5. ETHAN ZOHN

The *Survivor: Africa* winner was a collegiate goalkeeper at Vassar College, and like Shue went on to play in Zimbabwe for Highlanders FC. Zohn then took his winnings on *Survivor* and created Grassroots Soccer, an organization whose mission is to fight the AIDS epidemic in Africa. Zohn has also hosted a variety of soccer shows, the latest being *FC Fox* on the Fox Soccer Channel.

6. GAVIN ROSSDALE

These days, the former Bush front man is better known as Mr. Gwen Stefani. But aside from music, Rossdale's abiding passion was soccer, trying out for Chelsea as a teenager. When that didn't work out, Rossdale reportedly played in the semi-professional ranks before embarking on his music career. And while he clearly made the right choice, his soccer dream took on another form when he played English legend Stan Mortensen in the David Anspaugh film *The Game of Their Lives.*

7. STEVE NASH

Soccer runs deep in the blood of the two-time NBA MVP. Nash spent considerable amounts of his childhood playing the game, and his younger brother, Martin, is a member of the Canadian national team. But even after he chose the hardwood over the soccer field, the elder Nash has maintained his ties to the game. He is a devout fan of EPL side Tottenham Hotspur, and recently became an investor in Women's Professional Soccer, the successor league to the WUSA that will begin play in 2009.

8. JULIO IGLESIAS

The international pop star is reported to have been a stellar athlete in his youth, playing goalkeeper for the Real Madrid youth team. A severe car accident in 1963 left Iglesias partially paralyzed for more than eighteen months. The accident forced Iglesias to give up on his athletic dreams, but during his convalescence he learned to play the guitar, which proved to be the catalyst for his musical career.

9. **ROD STEWART**

While the Scottish singer maintains that music was his first love, soccer was a close second, as Stewart served as an apprentice for the London-based Brentford Football Club as a teenager. Such was his affinity for soccer that even after his career took off Stewart would sprinkle soccer references into his songs, including his ode to Celtic FC in the song "You're In My Heart."

Stewart still plays to this day in over-35 leagues in England and California, and even has his own soccer field, which he maintains with an irrigation system and full-time gardener that costs him $50,000 a year to maintain.

10. **GORDON RAMSAY**

Before he was berating wannabe chefs, Ramsay was being hammered by legendary Rangers manager Jock Wallace. Ramsay was an aspiring left back in his younger days, and even made two first-team appearances with the Glasgow side. But a nasty knee injury slowed his progress, and after a single season he was let go. Soon after, Ramsay took his first catering course, but the lessons he learned on the soccer field stayed with him. "I suppose I wouldn't be where I am today had [Rangers] not been so ruthless," Ramsay told the *Guardian*.

Soccer Cinema

Soccer has served as the vehicle for numerous films, and the game's increased traction in the United States has seen that trend accelerate. Yet the Beautiful Game has not necessarily translated into beautiful cinema, and there have been a scant few that would get the thumbs up from Ebert and Roeper.

1. *HARRY THE FOOTBALLER* (1911)

If you find yourself cursing the likes of *Soccer Dog: The Movie* then you can blame this film, believed to be the progenitor of all soccer movies. Made in 1911, the film features veteran actor Hay Plumb as a star player who is kidnapped by the opposition, only to be rescued by his girlfriend just in time for him to score the winning goal in the big game. The cliché-meter only went up from here.

2. *GOAL! THE DREAM BEGINS* (2005)

As close to the gold standard of soccer movies as you can get, the first installment of the *Goal!* trilogy managed to succeed where others had failed in that the action shots looked at least a bit realistic. Even Kuno Becker, who plays the role of the film's protagonist, Santiago Munez, managed to look like a reasonable approximation of a soccer player. Of course, cameos by numerous professionals, including several members of Newcastle United, helped immensely. Otherwise, the film is a standard, rags-to-riches story, but the attention to detail managed to grab the viewer in a way few other soccer films have.

3. *BEND IT LIKE BECKHAM* (2002)

More a coming-of-age film rather than a pure soccer movie, it tells the story of a Sikh teenager growing up in London who would rather play soccer than follow the traditional upbringing espoused by her parents. Light on game action but strong on story and characters, the movie grossed over $75 million worldwide, the most of any soccer movie to date.

4. *ESCAPE TO VICTORY* (1981)

Also known by its shorter title of *Victory*, the movie is about Allied POWs who play an exhibition match against a German All-Star team, and who use the match as a means of escaping, but not before giving their captors everything they can handle on the field. With Pelé mumbling his lines and the sight of Sylvester Stallone (all five-foot-six of him) playing in goal, the film falls short. Michael Caine played the part of the coach, and several other notable players, including Argentine World Cup-winner Ossie Ardiles, also appeared in the film.

More compelling is the story upon which the movie is based. According to legend, During World War II, Ukrainian players living in Kiev during the Nazi occupation formed a team that went undefeated against Axis opposition, but it was to prove costly. In a game known as "The Death Match," the team, comprised mostly of players from Dynamo Kiev, defeated their German opponents 5-3. The players were later arrested and sent to a labor camp on suspicion that they were members of the Soviet secret police, the NKVD, and five were later executed. Many have questioned the authenticity of the story, but a statue in honor of the deceased players was eventually erected outside of the Zenit Stadium where the match took place.

5. *THE GAME OF THEIR LIVES* (2005)
Also known as *The Miracle Match*, the movie tells the story of the United States's epic 1-0 victory over England in the 1950 World Cup. And you'd think that an upset as monumental as this one would make for a great movie. It didn't. In fact the most enduring image of the film is Ed McIlvenney, played by none other than one-time U.S. captain John Harkes, bellowing "Codswallop!" several times at the end of the film.

A better choice would be the documentary of the same name that chronicles the experiences of North Korea's national team during the 1966 World Cup.

6. *MEAN MACHINE* (2001)
The soccer version of *The Longest Yard* sees former Wimbledon defender Vinnie Jones take a star turn as Danny Meehan, an English international who is banned for life for throwing a game against Germany, and then is jailed for assault. Meehan then leads the cons against the guards with predictable, if entertaining results. As credible as Jones's performance is, the show is stolen by Jason Statham, who plays Monk, the cons' psychotic goalkeeper, as well as the hilarious commentating duo of Jeff Innocent and Jake Abraham, known in the film as Bob and Bob.

7. *MIKE BASSETT: ENGLAND MANAGER* (2001)
This film is to soccer what *Spinal Tap* is to music, as its

"mockumentary" format skewers the game and all its trappings to the bone. Ricky Tomlinson plays the part of a bumbling coach who becomes manager of the English national team because no one else will take the job, and the spoofs of various players and media members are as accurate as a perfectly weighted through ball.

8. *FEVER PITCH* (1997)

While the American version focused on a fan's obsession with the Boston Red Sox, this version is truer to the book of the same name, with Colin Firth playing the role of Paul Ashworth, whose obsession with Arsenal is his only lasting relationship, much to the dismay of love-interest Sarah. Perhaps the line of the movie is when Sarah alleges that Paul can't commit, to which he responds of course he can. He's been an Arsenal fan for twenty years.

9. *GREEN STREET HOOLIGANS* (2005)

This film shows the other side of fandom, as it focuses on the hooligan element surrounding the game. Elijah Wood stars as an American sucked into the hooligan culture, doing about as much fighting in this film as he did in *The Lord of the Rings*. Despite the inherent violence, the movie does a credible job of showing some of the inherent contradictions of hooliganism.

10. *THE OTHER FINAL* (2003)

This documentary focuses on a match played between the two worst teams in the world, Bhutan and Montserrat, on the same day as the 2002 World Cup final. The match was dreamed up by Dutchman Johan Kramer after the Netherlands were eliminated from World Cup qualifying, and he crafts a remarkable story of the players, coaches, and administrators involved, showing that inspiration can be drawn from even the most humble of soccer dreams.

Celebrations

"Best Choreography" is an award usually reserved for the Oscars, not the soccer field, but there have been more than a few goal celebrations whose originality can't be questioned. Their good taste? That's another topic altogether.

1. CUAUHTÉMOC BLANCO

The Mexican's typical celebration, where he bends down on one knee in a traditional Aztec pose, is an ode to his namesake, one of the last Aztec leaders. But his most creative bit of merriment came during a match between Blanco's Club America and bitter rivals Chivas. After netting a penalty kick, Blanco took off his shoes, and like a matador, used them as swords to "stab" a hunched-over teammate in the back. The move was nicknamed "The Banderillero."

2. BERNARDO CORRADI

The Manchester City forward had been enduring a long barren spell in front of goal, but after finally breaking through in a November 2006 match against Fulham, he decided that something special was in order. Corradi ran over to the corner flag, pulled it up, and like a modern day King Arthur

Chicago Fire midfielder Cuauhtémoc Blanco strikes his
signature pose after scoring in the first half of the game between
Kansas City and the Fire on August 25, 2007. This is one of
several goal celebrations made famous by Blanco over the
years. *Tracy Allen/isiphotos.com*

proceeded to "knight" a procession of teammates, the first
one being none other than serial bad-boy Joey Barton. "If
[Barton] gets a knighthood before me, I'm leaving the
game," Manchester City manager Stuart Pearce later told
the *Independent*.

3. TIM CAHILL

As Corradi proved, the corner flag can be a valuable prop for goal celebrations, but during the 2005–06 EPL season, Cahill went for a simpler approach, using the flag as a sparring partner after scoring for club side Everton. The move gained a worldwide audience at the 2006 World Cup when Cahill scored Australia's first-ever World Cup goal and finished it off with his trademark celebration.

4. REAL MADRID

During the 2005–06 Spanish league season, the team's Brazilian contingent took to impersonating animals whenever one of them scored a goal. The players imitated a horse and a frog, but the one that drew the most ire was the "cockroach" routine, where the players would lie on their backs and wiggle their arms and legs in the air. Needless to say, the stunt went over about as well as a real cockroach invading Christmas dinner. After witnessing the celebration, Alaves owner Dmitry Piterman called the players "circus clowns." Real Madrid forward Ronaldo later claimed the stunt was dreamt up as part of a bet with two friends, who agreed to go to a restaurant dressed as women if the forward performed the celebration in a game. No word on whether Ronaldo's friends actually went through with their cross-dressing dare.

5. CLINT DEMPSEY

Back when the Fulham forward was plying his trade in MLS, he was known as much for his celebrations as he was for his breathtaking goals. Among the more famous of Dempsey's antics was when he mimed hitting a homerun against D.C. United. The reason? United were sharing RFK Stadium at the time with Major League Baseball's Washington

Nationals, and Dempsey's celebration took place right where home plate normally resided.

6. FRANCISCO TOTTI

Bebeto's "Rock the Baby" celebration has endured so many repeats you'd think it had gone into syndication, so it was left to the Roma midfielder to come up with something new. After scoring in 2005 against arch-rivals Lazio, Totti ran to the sideline, stuffed a ball underneath his chest, laid down on his back, and with teammate turned obstetrician Sammy Kuffor at the ready, "delivered" the ball to his teammate. Totti concocted the celebration as in honor of his wife Ilary Blasi, who was pregnant at the time.

7. PETER CROUCH

At six-foot-seven, the words "Crouch" and "smooth" aren't normally associated with one another. But when Crouch busted out the Robot dance during a pre-World Cup friendly against Hungary in 2006, it created a sensation. Crouch first displayed his moves at a pre-tournament party hosted by teammate David Beckham, and sufficiently goaded by teammates he repeated the performance after scoring the clinching goal in England's 3-1 victory. It's thought that the celebration was a response to criticism from fans and media that Crouch was robotic in his movements. The Liverpool forward has since stated that the celebration will now be reserved "for special occasions only."

8. ALECKO ESKANDARIAN

Back in 2006, the MetroStars of MLS were purchased by Austrian beverage giant Red Bull, who proceeded to re-christen the team the New York Red Bulls. That got Eskandarian thinking, and when he scored against the renamed team that season, the then-D.C. United forward ran to the sidelines, took a conspicuous swig of Red Bull, and proceeded to spit it out on the ground. MLS, showing no sense of humor at all, fined Eskandarian $250 for his display.

9. AHN JUNG-HWAN

The South Korean's late equalizer against the United States at the 2002 World Cup saw Ahn and his teammates mimic the moves of a speedskater. The celebration was a protest over the disqualification during the 2002 Winter Olympics of their countryman, Kim Dong-Sung, who was bounced from the 1500-meter short track speedskating event after colliding with American Apolo Anton Ohno. Ahn went on to even greater fame later in the tournament when his golden goal eliminated Italy in the second round.

10. STEPHEN IRELAND

After scoring on a thumping volley against Sunderland in a 2007–08 EPL match, Ireland celebrated with his Manchester City teammates by dropping his shorts to reveal underpants adorned with a Superman logo. In a remarkable show of restraint, the normally staid English F.A. decided to let Ireland off with a warning.

Bibliography

BOOKS

Anthony, Andrew. *On Penalties.* London: Yellow Jersey Press, 1999.

Clough, Brian. *Cloughie: Walking on Water.* London: Headline Book Publishing, 2002.

Galeano, Eduardo. *Soccer in Sun and Shadow.* London and New York: Verso, 1998.

———. *Voices in Time: A Life in Stories.* New York: Picador, 2007.

Gray, Andy. *Flat Back Four: The Tactical Game.* London: Macmillan Publishers Ltd.,1999.

Hunt, Chris, editor. *The Complete Book of Soccer.* Buffalo, NY: Firefly Books Ltd., 2006.

Jose, Colin. *American Soccer League: 1921–1931.* Lanham, MD and London: Scarecrow Press Inc., 1998.

———. *North American Soccer League Encyclopedia*, Haworth, NJ: St. Johann Press, 2003.

Kuper, Simon. *Soccer Against the Enemy.* London: The Orion Publishing Group, 1994, 2006.

Markovits, Andrei S. and Steven L. Hellerman. *Offside: Soccer and American Exceptionalism*, Princeton, NJ: Princeton University Press, 2001.

Miller, Clark. *He Always Puts It to the Right*. London: Orion Books, Ltd., 1998.

Radnedge, Keir, ed. *The Ultimate Encyclopedia of Soccer*. London: Carlton Books Ltd., 2002.

Tossell, Dave. *Playing for Uncle Sam*. Edinburgh and London: Mainstream Publishing, 2003.

Toye, Clive. *A Kick in the Grass*. Haworth, NJ: St. Johann Press, 2006.

Winner, David. *Brilliant Orange: The Neurotic Genius of Dutch Football*. London: Bloomsbury Publishing, 2000.

MAGAZINES

Soccer America, 1982–2008

WEBSITES

The BBC, http://www.bbc.co.uk

ESPN Soccernet, http://soccernet.espn.go.com

FIFA.com, http://www.fifa.com

The Guardian, http://www.guardian.co.uk

The Independent, http://www.independent.co.uk

The Official Website of Major League Soccer, http://www.mlsnet.com

Rec.Sport.Soccer Statistics Foundation, http://www.rsssf.com

Soccer America, http://www.socceramerica.com

Sports Illustrated, http://sportsillustrated.cnn.com

The Times Online, http://www.timesonline.co.uk

UEFA.com, http://www.uefa.com

U.S. Soccer Official Website, www.ussoccer.com

Index

Muller, Gerd, 84, 85
Mullinix, Siri, 67
Muratti, 103–104
Mutu, Adrian, 197

Namibian Cup, 209
Nash, Steve, 244
Neeskens, Johan, 3, 84
Nelsen, Ryan, 60
Nesta, Alessandro, 155
Netherlands, 74, 84, 87–89, 127
Neville, Gary, 140, 218
New Bedford Whalers, 10
New England Revolution, 48–49, 52
New York Cosmos, 13, 20, 212–213
New York/New Jersey Metro-Stars, 50–51, 52, 57, 62, 63, 64
New York Power, 68
Newman, Ron, 14, 15, 16
Noha, Mike, 10–11
Nordby, Bente, 66
North American Soccer League, 3–4, 13–18
Northern Ireland, 76, 110, 125
Nottingham Forest F.C., 229–230
Nowak, Peter, 58

O'Brien, John, 32
Oforiquaye, Peter, 113
Olisadebe, Emmanuel, 186–187
Olsen, Jesper, 136

Onzari, Cesareo, 136
Ordenewitz, Frank, 232
Other Final, The, 249–250
Owen, Michael, 155, 215
Ozcan, Ozgurcan, 231

Pagliuca, Gianluca, 86, 155
Paisley Panda, 240
Palermo, Martin, 204, 206
Palop, Andres, 145
Parkhurst, Michael, 231–232
Parlow, Cindy, 68
Panenka, Antonin, 208–209
Patenaude, Bert, 10
Pekerman, Jose, 89
Pelé, 3, 13–14, 19, 110, 111, 120, 124, 185, 209
Pele, Abedi, 77
Peladão, The, 104
Pellie the Elephant, 238–239
penalty kick, 205–209
Penarol, A.C., 121
Pereira de Carvalho, Edilson, 222–223
Petke, Mike, 190
Pepe, 120
Philadelphia Ukrainian Nationals, 10, 11
Piterman, Dmitry, 171, 253
Portugal, 85–86, 103
Power, Karl, 217
Pozzo, Vittorio, 176, 184
Prosinecki, Robert, 188
Pusatch, Anatoli, 152
Puskás, Ferenc, 82–83, 129, 187

About the Author

It was back in 1978 that Jeff Carlisle attended his first soccer game, an NASL match between his hometown Ft. Lauderdale Strikers and the Chicago Sting. He has been hooked on the beautiful game ever since.

Since 2005, Carlisle has been a regular contributor to ESPN's Soccernet website, and was among the site's main writers during the 2006 World Cup as well as the 2007 Copa America, providing extensive coverage of the U.S. men's national team. Carlisle also covers Major League Soccer for ESPN, and has written numerous articles about the league's teams and players.

Carlisle lives in Menlo Park, California, with his wife Andréa and son Ben.